D1030917

the art of
pastoral
conversation

the art of
pastoral
conversation

Heije Faber and
Ebel van der Schoot

ABINGDON PRESS
new york   nashville

HET PASTORALE GESPREK

© 1962 Erven J. Bijleveld, Utrecht, Holland

THE ART OF PASTORAL CONVERSATION

Translation © 1965 by Abingdon Press

Library of Congress Catalog Card Number: 65-21977

To our American teachers in the field of pastoral psychology—and especially to Simon Doniger, Seward Hiltner, Paul W. Pruyser, and Robert R. Wright, without whose help the publication of this book would not have been possible

introduction

It is my belief, and my hope, that this book begins a new era in European theological scholarship. In the classic fields of theology an American would have to be provincial indeed to deny the eminence and relevance of the big B's: Barth and Brunner, and Bultmann, to say nothing of Eichrodt and von Rad, and many others. We must also concede pioneering in new fields, such as by van der Leeuw, Wach, and Eliade in the history of religions (even if the last two did come eventually to the United States). What I never expected in my lifetime was any European who would get down to "conversation," quite literally, in pastoral work. Happily, Faber and van der Schoot hereby prove me wrong. They leave me in their debt and, if American ministers can get over their reluctance to be taught by Dutchmen, I think they will join me in my gratitude.

Since my contacts with the American frontier have never been sanded away, I am torn between astonishment and incredulity that two Reformed ministers in Holland, of all places, should be able to take a lead that began in the United States (analysis of actual literal pastoral conversations), pursue it with such clarity and penetration, and above all interpret within it the clear (once explained) theological significance. It is on the last point—which we greatly need—that their European strength is most apparent. And yet, unlike other previous European writers, they do not assume that attentiveness to actual, literal, concrete, and specific conversations is a regrettable by-product of American activism. They take concreteness seriously. Indeed, they have done us one better, for they can find theological significance in a conversation bounded by spinach and a shopkeeper at one end and a housewife and grocery cart at the other.

This book is one of the most immediately and practically helpful works for the pastor that has been published for many years. And if a few psychiatrists and other physicians, social workers, psychologists, educational counselors, and others—whose basic method of dealing with people is "conversation"—would also read it, I believe it just might illuminate their insights. But it is, without apology, pastorally slanted. How can we converse helpfully with our people? How can we analyze what it is we are doing in conversation, not only in our pastoral counseling but also in the many kinds of contacts, relatively formal or otherwise, that we have? How can we be ourselves, and still be responsible in our conversations? To all such questions this book is the best answer that current knowledge makes available. And it is highly readable.

Conversation, by any definition, is the stuff of human communication. It is never words alone, but in human life it is seldom wholly without words. What do the words (and the tone, the inflection, the pauses, the grunts, and the rough breathings) convey to the other? And what does the return (whether words, grunts, or rough breathings) say back to the starter of the process? Does it perform its proper *human* function—getting the housewife off spinach and on to green beans when spinach is too expensive, moving the pale and wan lover to a forthright declaration of his true feelings, promoting a true "I-Thou" encounter when it is humanly appropriate, or getting off the elevator at the right floor, when "I-Thou" relationships would only confuse the operator? Communication is for many legitimate purposes; conversation is its instrument. Analysis of conversation, and command of the principles for such analysis, may come in just as handily in the supermarket as by the hospital bed. It is such principles that the authors make available, of course, with a clear bias in favor of the implication of the principles for pastoral care.

Heije Faber (who is a teacher at Leyden, as well as a doctor) came to the United States five years ago to study our work in pastoral care and clinical training. I had the good fortune to be one of his hosts. His remarkably penetrating observations on his American visit, and his analysis of the European situation in pastoral care in the light of it, were published in the small volume *Pastoral Care and Clinical Training in America,* which is at the same time the best support and critique of our entire American movement that has yet been published. In the present volume Dr. Faber neither praises nor criticizes us. He simply takes our lead, and shows us where it proceeds. The result is penetrating, stimulating, eminently practical, and theologically illuminating whatever the reader's brand of theology.

Although I have not had the pleasure of meeting Dr. van der Schoot in person, we have engaged in long correspondence, and this in itself has proved to be genuine conversation. Like Faber, van der Schoot has had excellent psychological training but also orients himself and his concerns in a theological context.

The Dutch edition of this book was first called to my attention by my Menninger Foundation colleague, Dr. Paul W. Pruyser. In view of his warm commendation and with a boost from a possible publisher, I recommended an English translation and American publication; and, after a lot of hard extra work on the part of Drs. Faber and van der Schoot, and remarkable editorial acumen on the part of Robert Roy Wright, the present book finally emerged. I am proud and delighted to have played some part in this translative process; for translation is more than literal words—it is also the communication, through "conversation," of a spirit.

The American reader should take seriously the authors' remarks about their hesitation to have this book appear in English and in America. Their writing intent was clearly toward the Continent. But I, among others, felt, and still feel, that precisely this patience with many previously scornful of the "concrete" makes their book peculiarly important in the United States. Their way of getting at the subject is both imaginative and refreshing. And they have more novelty than they have admitted. "Pastoral conversation" is, after all, nearly the whole mode of our ministry. We Americans cannot beat the Dutch in putting our finger on essentials. But we can profit from their fingers.

Seward Hiltner
Princeton Theological Seminary
1965

preface

A conversation is a subject demanding thorough reflection. It is the most obvious form of communication in which people are able to have a personal relationship with each other, yet at the same time it has apparently become a difficult business. This is so in conversations carried on spontaneously in everyday life and also holds good in every profession where conversation plays an important part. It is becoming more and more clear nowadays that to allow the way in which we carry out a conversation to depend only on intuition and common sense is no longer a responsible attitude. Both theoretical and practical training are indispensable.

When we deal with conversations and conversing, we are, on the one hand, involved with the psychology of the conversation in general terms as well as in its practical application. But on the other hand, we are also involved with a definite relationship which gives the conversation its special character. This book is about the psychology of conversations and the special nature of the pastoral conversation. It so happens that both authors of this book came to study psychology because of their particular interest in problems arising from questions of pastoral care in present-day society. We want to serve as pastoral psychologists in a rapidly changing world. When writing we have had the minister and his work continually in mind, yet we suppose that many another person who in his dedication to the gospel mission carries out similar conversations can learn something from this book, too. That is to say, it should be of interest to those who hold some position or function in the church (member of the church council, parish workers, deaconesses, church social workers, youth leaders, etc.) and those who while working in other professions feel the desire to bring God's word into them.

After the Dutch edition of this book was published, we were encouraged by Paul W. Pruyser, who reviewed it in *Pastoral Psychology*, and by other American friends to have it translated and published in the United States. At first, we were reluctant to do so. This book was a first attempt in a European country to stimulate interest in the problems of pastoral conversations and the possibilities contained in the "clinical training" movement. This is a movement, however, which is widely known in America, and many American pastors have participated in it.

A part of our reluctance was overcome by the encouragement we received from our American friends. We have the impression that just because this book was written for a European public, it may have a certain interest for American readers. We hope that the European climate of opinion and point of view which is developed in this book will perhaps add a few points to the American discussion. We shall be very interested to see how readers with a different background from our own will react to this book. It is our opinion that in the field of pastoral training and work an exchange of experiences and points of view could be particularly fruitful.

In preparing the book for publication in America we have given it a slightly altered focus. Those parts which urged the importance of clinical training have been largely deleted, and the main emphasis of the book now rests on "the art of pastoral conversation." The present edition has five chapters written by Dr. Faber, chapters 1-5, and four by Dr. van der Schoot, chapters 6-9. We hope that, in its present form, the book will be a contribution to the movement for better pastoral education, which is quickly becoming worldwide.

We offer our grateful thanks to all those who have helped us with the translation and publication of this book, our two translators in Holland, Mrs. C. A. Franken-Battershill (chapters 1-5) and Miss G. W. Abbink (chapters 6-9) and to Simon Doniger and Paul W. Pruyser in the United States. We owe an additional debt of gratitude to Dr. Seward Hiltner for his kindness in writing an introduction for this edition.

Heije Faber
Ebel van der Schoot

contents

the art of
pastoral
conversation

I

Conversation and the
Helping Professions

What is a conversation really? Superficially it is contact between people who exchange words. These words have a content, and one person appears to react to the content of the information given by the other. The housewife in a shop asks how much the spinach costs today, and the shopkeeper answers by telling her a certain price. So we can consider the conversation in this sense: we have spoken together about something, agreed about it, and made a decision. In this way we concentrate our attention on the content of the words spoken and the results consequent to the exchange of words.

However, on looking more closely we notice that even in this simple conversation between the housewife and the shopkeeper more has taken place, and of such radical importance that the exchange of words has undergone considerable change. What do you make of this? The housewife who asks the shopkeeper the price of the spinach is well known to him. She is the mother of a large family, and not at all well off. The spinach is still very expensive. Is it not possible that the man, out of a certain sympathy with the woman, will say something such as: "Fresh vegetables are still expensive—the weather hasn't helped. The spinach costs. . . ." Even that he would perhaps add, "But I've other nice vegetables"? And how about this situation? The man knows the customer as someone who likes to buy the newest and most expensive things but is slow about paying for them. Might he not say something such as: "I was only able to get hold of a small amount from the market and it's already been ordered by telephone for a dinner party"?

These examples show that in a conversation the content of the words is not only reacted to in a businesslike way, but that it calls up all sorts of associations and feelings in the listener, and that we react to the content of the words through these feelings. In the first instance, a feeling of sympathy colored the words used; in the second, a feeling of anxiety brought about a definite reaction which could not be accounted for objectively. Indeed, perhaps we could go further: even the question which was put by both women does not stand in isolation from certain feelings in the questioner.

It is quite likely that the first woman had asked the price of the spinach in some anxiety: "My husband does so like fresh vegetables, but won't they be too expensive? And if I ask the price and then don't buy the spinach, I'll seem such a fool." But the man has in some way followed her thoughts, or rather, has perhaps intuitively felt her difficulties, and he finds an answer—also the right tone of voice—which in spite of her disappointment she finds agreeable.

In the second conversation it is probable that the woman is suspicious anyway and expects that the man will offer some sort of excuse for not wanting to sell her fresh vegetables, so that it is practically certain that she will react to his answer with some sarcastic remark.

From these examples it is quite clear that the "extra" which we have just mentioned and which influences the choice of words—indeed, even the progress of a conversation—is to be found in the realm of the feelings. The opposite member in a conversation, his personality, and his words, do something to us. We are affected by them. We are involved with our feelings when coming into contact with another person.

In general this is not a bad thing. It makes life stimulating and colorful in that we let our feelings of happiness, sorrow, sympathy, dislike, love, or hate play a part in our contact with our fellow men. However, it is strange that we are not always conscious of how much our conversations with others are colored and determined by these emotions. Generally we only notice the content of the words themselves and forget that in both our conversational partner and ourselves the words work only within the context of certain feelings. We would get on much further if we did not always tend to forget that the success or failure of a conversation almost always depends not on our words but on our feelings.

Indeed, the whole study of "conversational techniques" has sprung from this. It is surprising to see how this study has progressed in various other fields during the last decades. I will only mention two books here which contain all sorts of worthwhile remarks for ministers. One comes from the world of the social worker: Ann Garrett's *Conversational Techniques: Basic Principles and Methods* [1] and *The Medical Interview,* that most instructive booklet by an Australian doctor, Ainslie Meares, which bears as sub-

---

[1] *Gesprekstechniek. Beginselen en Methoden* (Amsterdam: Sociale Academie).

title: "A study of clinically significant interpersonal reactions." It is recommended by the publisher[2] with the words: "Shows how to help patients by the simple procedure of talking with them." But everyone who is even slightly at home in this field and knows about leadership training in industry, experiments with new methods in education, and other developments, realizes that everything depends on this more profound understanding of what a conversation really is and on contact between people.

From here to the pastoral conversation is but a short step. One can indeed state that the new interest in problems of pastoral conversations is characterized by the fact—which people involved in this work are conscious of, also—that with a one-sided emphasis on the content of the verbal exchange, one gets nowhere, that often apparently something is missing in the pastoral contact as such and that this makes the proper working of the gospel message, the kerygma, impossible. It would be well worth while to find out what factors have combined here to produce this state of emergency—for in many cases this word can be used. I have the impression that a drastic shift in our pattern of culture has played an important role here. I have written in some detail about this elsewhere, including in the collection *Pastoral Psychological Essays*.[3]

I should like to show by one example how the carrying out of a pastoral conversation—and thus its success or failure—does not depend only on the words which are exchanged but also on the feelings harbored by the two participants, both in respect to themselves and to each other.

During an analysis of such conversations which I was holding

[2] (Springfield, Ill.: Charles C. Thomas, 1957).
[3] *Pastoraal Psychologische Opstellen* (Den Haag: N. V. Het Boekencentrum, 1961).

recently with members of the clergy, one of them came forward with a practical example of his own which had more or less floored him. He worried about how this particular conversation could have taken the turn it did, and what conclusions he should draw about himself and the man with whom he had talked. He wondered whether this man was incorrigible or whether he himself had made a mistake somewhere which had made it impossible to get the right contact with this man.

This example is a talk with a well-to-do businessman who had withdrawn from his work and, the minister thought, lived a very egocentric life. He was someone who more or less lived for his car, his garden, and a well-appointed house. He was married— without children—to a woman who had recently been ill (the minister had frequently visited her) and who had now been taken to a psychiatric home where it was most likely that she would have to stay for the rest of her life. The man had not been a bad husband to her, but according to the minister was not sufficiently moved by the pathetic fate of his wife. About a month after the wife had gone, the minister paid a call on the husband, who complained of the emptiness of the house and of his life. To this the minister reacted with these words: "You could get rid of this emptiness if you tried both to do and be something for other people." The man's answer was: "Catch me!"

We will not discuss now what the minister, who was shocked by this answer, had said further but try to find out, as we did at the time, what actually took place in this fairly ordinary pastoral situation. Most clergy will recognize similar conversations from their own experience. If one pays attention only to the words spoken in this example, one has to conclude that here is a particularly obdurate character. The minister himself had, after some hesitation, come to this pessimistic conclusion. It is, however, noticeable that the group who had time to analyze the talk quietly with their colleague arrived at a completely different conclusion. Later, the minister himself agreed with this.

We began the analysis from the point of view, developed above, that not only the words but the feelings behind them are important, and we attempted to reconstruct the emotional atmosphere with the help of the minister. We first asked ourselves what feelings had played a role on the minister's side when he had spoken. We arrived at the following:

In the first place: this man needs advice.

In the second place: this man is self-centered.

In the third place: his wife had suffered from this.

In the fourth place: somehow I must bring this home to him.

When we went into the question of what sort of feelings lay behind the man's words, we very easily arrived at the following:

Firstly: this minister wants to push me into a certain position.

Secondly: I never asked for this, and I shall react negatively to this interference.

Thirdly: in both the words and the tone of voice there is a sound of reproof.

And lastly: this minister is not standing next to me or behind me but in opposition to me.

Our conclusion was that given this set of feelings one could only expect the man to reject the approach made to him. Indeed, we went so far as to wonder whether by using the words he did in a clearly negative reaction, he had not in fact sent up a distress signal ("Catch me!" meaning "I have had so many rotten experiences with fellow men") to which the minister could have made a positive comeback so that the talk might have been turned into a fruitful direction. In the next chapter I will raise the question of how the minister could have saved the situation. I only want to emphasize here that in pastoral conversations it is not the words spoken but rather the feelings which both partners possess and show (or perhaps hide!) that determine the development of the conversation; and that the one who is leading the conversation—here the minister—must be expected to pay attention to this.

How this can be accomplished I hope to be able to make clear in the pages of this book.

II

Listening and Response
in Pastoral Conversation

We may conclude from our first "reconnaisance" in the field of conversation in general, and pastoral conversation in particular, that in "listening and response" the secret of a good conversation is hidden. Carl Rogers is one of the men who, over the years, has explored this secret of conversation most fruitfully. In order to clarify both the structure and the problems of pastoral contact, I propose to examine a number of ideas and conceptions with which he works and which—so to speak—form his "system," although his method has never been a static thing but has developed across the years. I refer particularly to his *client-centered therapy*, without committing either him to a final position or myself to accepting uncritically everything he has said.

Indeed, it should be emphasized that one cannot really speak of a system or even a method in connection with Rogers. His method or system, or what perhaps one can better call his technique, is primarily an aid to bring about a good relationship between the psychotherapist and his client. Over the years the main emphasis of his work and thought has come to rest on this relationship; on the care, openheartedness, trust, and love on the psychotherapist's part and on the reaction to this on the part of the client. It is a mistake, which unfortunately is still sometimes made in official psychotherapeutic circles, to emphasize Rogers' technique of "reflection," or to explain away as a deficiency in Christian sympathy his conviction that a certain distance must be maintained by the therapist from his client. He is in fact always pleading for a warm and loving relationship. I can understand that some psychotherapeutic circles harbor objections against clinical psychology in Rogers' definition—I can even agree with some of these—but these objections must be made on other premises; for example, on his absolute refusal of diagnosis and interpretation, and so, too, of the indications of what sort of cure is necessary.

Likewise, we must not forget that Rogers is a psychotherapist or clinical psychologist and not a pastor, even though because of his original preference for theology a number of religious ideas play a role in his thought. His attitude to his clients, however, is concerned with their health and not with their relationship with God. He is a counselor, and in a certain sense a doctor, but not a minister. Therefore, the point of this chapter is not to show that pastoral work would be helped if we all became followers of Rogers, went counseling in his footsteps, and in so doing turned pastoral work into a sideline of psychotherapy. No, we only want to glance at the methods and ideas with which Rogers constructs his psychotherapeutic relationship and look more closely at the experience he gains, in order that we might return to the pastoral conversation better equipped to understand it. In a later chapter—I only mention it here to dispel any charges of one-sidedness—I want to consider the field of more orthodox psychotherapy to see what we can learn there for a greater understanding and more responsible way of going about pastoral conversing; that is to say, over and above what we have learned from Rogers.

Acceptance in Relationship

On page 113 of one of his first publications, *Counseling and Psychotherapy,* Rogers himself gives a clear description of his methods.

The counseling relationship is one in which warmth of acceptance and absence of coercion or personal pressure on the part of the counselor permits the maximum of expression of feelings, attitudes, and problems by the counselee. . . . In this unique experience of complete emotional freedom within a well defined framework the client is free to recognize and understand his impulses and patterns, positive and negative, as in no other relationship.[1]

The stress therefore lies on a good *relationship;* this is quite clear. In this relationship the client comes into the open and so attains a more healthy life. For the moment we shall leave aside the question of what relationship such a therapeutic method has to the work of pastoral care and ask with what ideas Rogers clarifies this relationship and what important points he develops for his kind of conversation, and thus also perhaps for a pastoral conversation.

One of the most important aspects of this method is that the therapist must be "nondirective" in his relationship to his client. I think it well that we be clearly aware from the start that Rogers uses this phrase in the framework of a therapeutic relationship. What he means by nondirective is aimed at those schools of psycho-

[1] (Boston: Houghton Mifflin Company, 1942).

therapy in which the therapist forms diagnoses and communicates interpretations of symptoms. Rogers rejects a relationship in which the client is turned into a patient and so turned into an object. On these grounds he also rejects a relationship in which the psychotherapist "moralizes" or "dogmatizes." The client must remain responsible for his own life, and so there must be no question of any sort of pressure or force, in however rough or refined a form.

The psychotherapist must accept the client as he is and must not let himself be led by any preconceived judgments. This is the "acceptance" which through the years Rogers has stressed more and more and which itself leads to the fact that a therapist must be nondirective, not moralizing nor dogmatizing, and must leave the freedom and responsibility of his existence in the hands of the other man and so by not turning him into an object by diagnosis or interpretation remain seeing him and experiencing him as a subject.

I am also perfectly certain that the pastor must begin from this position of acceptance, and that he must accept the consequences. I should indeed go so far as to suggest that Rogers' acceptance of the client—and indeed the entire medical position in respect of the patient—has its roots in the Christian acceptance in God's name of every man. However this acceptance is not the only aspect even though it is an essential, indispensable, and often sufficient aspect of the pastor's job. The pastor must also know himself to be the servant of Christ; like Jeremiah and Isaiah he has a prophetic assignment. He must summon and call. But we have already mentioned this point and will return to it later.

There are additional ideas and conceptions of Rogers which can help us in throwing light on the structure and problems of the pastoral conversation.

Reflection of Significant Feelings

Up till now we have approached the relationship of the psycho-therapist (and the pastor may be included in this term) to his client from a negative position, namely, that the psychotherapist must be nondirective. The question must now be asked: What does the psychotherapist do that is positive? Rogers indicates a special task for him which he defines as "reflection."

What is meant by this, and what is its use for pastoral conversations? The answer is fairly simple. If the therapist does not want to be directive but rather wants to stand by the other man in such a way that the man feels that he is accepted with a certain warmth and at the same time that he is understood, the therapist can achieve his aim by formulating anew his client's feelings which are often vague and expressed only after some resistance. Perhaps we can remember occasions in our youth when we found ourselves in front of one of our teachers or parents feeling guilty and frightened, without a clean good-conduct sheet. We listened then with hanging head to the voice of that person who only said, "You've been dishonest and you're sorry about it, but you're afraid I'm going to be angry." Then suddenly we felt that here was someone who understood us in our loneliness and because of that did not leave us in the lurch. What had this teacher or parent done? In reality nothing but "reflecting" the feeling which was there vaguely in us with real, yet at the same time reserved, sympathy. One cannot formulate precisely what happened at that moment, but in this way and in this relationship we lost the desire to defend ourselves. We dared to see our own faults and to acknowledge them and if necessary even to own up to them. In short, we were encouraged to react, not in a childish way, but as people who were responsible for their own actions, in a grown-up way.

I believe it is true to say that this is what Rogers understands under the term "psychotherapy." He himself says:

In the therapeutic experience to see one's own attitudes, confusions, ambivalences, feelings and perceptions accurately expressed by another, but stripped of their complications of emotion is to see oneself objectively, and paves the way for acceptance into the self of all those elements which are now more clearly perceived. Reorganization of the self and more integrated functioning of the self are thus furthered.[2]

The difference here with the conversation of our youth is, of course, that then we had said nothing, so that the other person could only formulate our feelings for us by empathy; while in a normal psychotherapeutic interview we would certainly have spoken. This difference teaches us one thing. Reflection is not simply saying in other words what the other man has already said, but it is penetrating into the feelings brought to the surface by him in such a way that they are reflected back to him.

Two ideas in common with this one are particularly important to Rogers. The first idea is *empathy*. That is to say, we penetrate the other man's feelings comprehendingly. With the help of a healthily reserved sympathy we project ourselves into him and concern ourselves particularly with his feelings. We do not look for any basic feeling but follow the changes and continuity of his emotions; the other person must have the certainty that we sympathize with him. Here we meet another idea—that which Rogers calls *the frame of reference*, the world of emotion and thought which the client expresses at a certain moment. Should we fall out of this frame of reference by not comprehending the other person

[2] *Client-Centered Therapy* (Boston: Houghton Mifflin Company, 1951), pp. 40-41.

sufficiently, he then feels himself not to be understood and the relationship is momentarily broken. In a good conversation this should right itself quickly, but if this stepping outside the frame of reference should happen too often or too obviously it can seriously endanger the success of the conversation. Rogers thinks that one of the faults of interpretation is connected with this point.

Thus, it is possible that the psychotherapist understands his client better than the client does. But he must not tell his client this because by so doing he will step outside the frame of reference, and the conversation, which is a dynamic process, will be interrupted. When the right moment comes, the client will see this point for himself, and that will be a liberating insight for him. By his opposition to all interpretation Rogers places himself in opposition to traditional psychotherapy, but he is consistent here. He maintains that by interpretation the personality of his client is violated, and this must never happen. We have already noted above that in our opinion Rogers is here too rigidly dogmatic. However, this principle seems right to me for a pastoral conversation; interpretation in the technical sense of the word is the work of a specialist, and the minister ought to keep away from it as much as possible.

An Example from Rogers

Before we go on to consider the question of how and how far we can use these ideas and concepts of Rogers in a pastoral conversation, we should like to illustrate by a single example what has been said up till now. In order to clarify the meaning of reflection with the connected ideas of empathy and the frame of reference I shall quote here part of a conversation which occurs in *Client-Centered Therapy.*

Cl(ient): I could see what I thought was needed in the situation and what was the idea I thought might be interjected to make people feel happy, and I'd do that.

Co(unselor): In other words, what you did was always in the direction of trying to keep things smooth and to make other people feel better and to smooth the situation.

Cl: Yes, I think that's what it was. Now the reason why I did it probably was—I mean, not that I was a good little Samaritan going around making other people happy, but that was probably the role that fell easiest for me to play. I'd been doing it around home so much. I just didn't stand up for my own convictions, until I don't know whether I have any convictions to stand up for.

Co: You feel that for a long time you've been playing the role of kind of smoothing out the frictions or differences or what not. . . .

Cl: M-hm.

Co: Rather than having any opinion or reaction of your own in the situation. Is that it?

Cl: That's it. Or that I haven't been really honestly being myself, or actually knowing what my real self is, and that I've been just playing a sort of false role. Whatever role no one else was playing, and that needed to be played at the time, I'd try to fill it in.

Co: Whatever kind of person that was needed to kinda help out that situation you'd be that kind of person rather than be anything original or deeply your own.[3]

Anyone carefully reading this fragment of a conversation which has been recorded on a tape and can thus be faithfully reproduced, will notice that the counselor follows his client. He stands next to him but in no way directs him. In this calm, thoughtful relationship the client arrives at a more profound understanding of himself. As sentence follows sentence more important material is

[3] p. 153.

dredged up about him. From this scrap we can clearly see what empathy consists of, and because of this empathy the counselor remains within the frame of reference. Right at the beginning, for instance, he could have said: "While you were so busy making the situation a pleasant one, you really weren't yourself. It was more or less a role you were playing." But by saying this he would have stepped outside the frame of reference and given an interpretation in which his client would have felt himself to have been judged and been treated not as a subject but as an object. He would have got the feeling that the counselor no longer stood with him but over against him, and that he had, so to speak, rejected him.

With this example before us it is not difficult to think up some reactions for the counselor which would somehow have been directive and thus rejected by Rogers. Here are a few examples. After the client's first sentence the counselor could have answered:

a. "You have to realize that in this way you are not paying enough attention to your own interests, and that you really ought not to let yourself be so exploited."

The answer in its present form is directive. The counselor applies a certain pressure to persuade the client into a direction which he thinks good for him; the freedom and sense of responsibility of the client are being neglected. The counselor seems to forget that the client bears the responsibility of his own life. In everyday speech, and in many a pastoral conversation, this is indeed often the position we take up in respect to others. It is clear that the flow of feelings would be completely broken here. Experience teaches us that this sort of advice makes the client argumentative; had the counselor remained nondirective, the client would have probably come to the same conclusion a few minutes later.

b. "So you are lacking in common or garden-variety self-respect."

This is a diagnosis. The counselor stands in opposition to his client; he no longer thinks or feels with him but has turned him into an object of research and now divulges the results of his discoveries. It is at this point, as we have seen above, that Rogers is unneccessarily dogmatic in relation to the methods of orthodox psychotherapy. Such a diagnosis *can* be given in such a way that the relationship is not broken, and is perhaps even deepened. However, this is then the typical doctor-patient relationship, the specialist against the helpless. It is just this relationship that Rogers will not accept; he works from a belief in the integrating power of the client himself. The question then is: Does everyone who is in need of psychotherapy have enough inner strength? Or, in the case of certain patients, does not the way to this strength have to be paved first with specialist aid, such as interpretation, suggestion, and even hypnosis?

Be this as it may, it is clear that in Rogers' way of thinking in this case the flow of feelings is broken and the relationship disturbed.

c. "This kind of thing seems to me to be a sign of immaturity."

One could call this an interpretation; it occupies a part of the diagnostic position. Everything which we have noted about *b* is applicable here.

d. "Isn't it really wrong to think so little about yourself?"

The counselor wants to help his client and here begins to moralize. Here, too, the flow of feelings is broken. The client will probably feel slightly irritated that he cannot go on talking but instead is, with his feelings, just pushed aside. However well meant, the subject-subject relationship is lost, and once more the client feels himself to be the object of a judgment—this time a moral one. The conversation gets stuck and when it revives takes a turn in a very different direction, from which it will generally be impossible to redirect it back onto its old course. This is in fact the same situation as the one we quoted in Chapter 1, and we must be prepared for a negative reply. It is also noticeable that such a reaction always leads to a similar negative reaction on the part of the pastor, which results in the conversation inevitably turning into a discussion and becoming pastorally unproductive. Getting involved in a discussion in a pastoral conversation is a sure sign that the right sort of contact has been lost. The pastor is no more with the other, and there is no longer any question of standing by him.

e. "What should one really call this? Love of one's neighbor or a subtle sort of self-love?"

This is a form of dogmatizing. The minister here is really beginning a discussion of how such behavior should be regarded from a religious point of view. Indeed, this is an important problem and might be a good thing to discuss with someone, but not in a pastoral conversation such as this. The flow of feelings is interrupted; the other man feels himself rejected and becomes irritated. His desire to go on talking cools, and his hope that this conversation will mean something to him disappears. Moreover, he senses in this question a hidden and, at this stage of the conversation, unfitting reprimand.

Rogerian Counseling and the Pastor

I hope that Rogers' method or system is by now sufficiently clear. I want now to attempt to outline its worth for pastoral conversations.

From this exposition we can see that this method tries to help the client by building up a warm subject-subject relationship, one which comes into its own by the counselor holding a nondirective position and using a technique to reflect feelings. The client thus experiences a prop and stay until he is inwardly ready to face himself. We must not forget that Rogers emphatically speaks of a method of psychotherapy. We will not discuss the objections that can be made against it from the psychotherapeutic side. We accept it as an important point of view about the conducting of a conversation, in which one person is helping the other. How much can Rogers help us? This is the question that we must now look at.

We have given some examples above of pastoral care in its purest form. Christ's exhortation to conversion, Jeremiah's warning, and Deutero-Isaiah's message of consolation are all aspects of what we understand as pastoral care, and as such are examples of pastoral conversing of one man with another. They want to help their fellow men see that they, too, are standing in God's light. We have shown that some important characteristics of pastoral care and thus of pastoral conversations are clearly brought up here. In this pastoral care there is no moralizing nor dogmatizing, and no form of pushing. The other man is a subject to whom something is said which he is free to accept or reject. The prophet is not the expert but a humble servant of the great Messenger, who has prepared himself for his work with an inward devotion. He does not set himself apart from the other man or his people, but he lives among them and intensely with them, even when he has to call them to repentance. So for them, too, the basis on which they build their work is empathy.

Is there anything else to say about that which happens in pastoral care, in these pastoral contacts? I would like to discuss more completely the points in which this contact can be compared with the psychotherapeutic contact as Rogers sees it.

Let us establish right from the beginning that any original dimension of pastoral contact is missing in the Rogers' type of conversation. Pastoral care is clearly something different from psychotherapy. Yet even at first sight there are some things which correspond: a subject-subject relationship, being nondirective (not moralizing, pushing, etc.), and, as Rogers describes it, standing beside the other man.

It seems to me clear from the examples given that pastoral care is not only the task of delivering a message—the simile of Barth's that being a minister is like being a postman comes to mind here—but also the task of meeting the messenger. The man who brings the message has taken on himself a responsibility for the others to whom he brings it; he suffers with them or because of them—in short, he functions for love of them. And he who listens to the message comes just as much under the grip of this love as of the message itself. In the figure of Christ in Christology it is impossible to differentiate between the prophet, priest, or king. Jeremiah often shows symbolically that he suffers among his people, and, as it were, seals his work with his imprisonment. Nor is it chance that in the stories about him most of the attention was paid to this side of his life.

We also see that in the emotional life of a prophet he not only behaves as he does because of a need to speak, to be a teacher, but because of this love. Many are the words of Christ that make this clear. He weeps over Jerusalem; he will give his life for her. And the joy expressed in Isaiah 40 is only to be understood in the fact that here is a man who loves his people passionately and who has suffered their sorrows wholeheartedly for years.

My proposition is this, that in this contact the message and the messenger are not to be divided, and that the effect of the message depends not only on the chance telling of it, but also on the fact that it is this messenger who brings it. That Christ not only told sinners that the kingdom was meant for them, too, but that he ate and went about with them, showing that the message was part of a special relationship, influenced the effect of his work. Would Zacchaeus have dared to believe the message of Christ had Christ not also told him his intention of sitting at table with him? Would the preaching and exhortation of Paul have made such an impression if the man behind the message had not suffered for it and for his community in many ways? I am convinced that the love which inspires a prophet to his preaching results in his finding a hearing. He is not an expert, a teacher who communicates some insight or knowledge, but to those to whom he speaks he is as one who would go through fire for them. I offer the suggestion that this which we in dogmatics call the "*testimonium spiritus sancti*" viewed psychologically connects up with this fact.

The inner freedom which the message brings about, the acceptance that one is standing in the beam of God's light, is not only due to the words themselves but to the fact that these words are spoken in a very special relationship—one which is characterized by love. Indeed, it is possible that the relationship itself without words can achieve this liberation. The story of Zacchaeus is a perfect example of this.

In a more profound sense the prophet is, of course, directive. He indicates a certain line of direction; he offers us his diagnosis; he passes judgment. But it is not experienced as directive in Rogers' sense of the word, because in this relationship it has a liberating rather than imprisoning result. The prophet stands close to the other man, not opposite him; indeed, in his own belief perhaps he stands below him. When the other man or his people experience the relationship in another way—and of course this can happen—then all the same symptoms that arise when a conversation takes a directive turn in Rogers' terminology appear. People get irritated, cut themselves off, turn their backs, regard everything as unasked for interference, and silence him. At this point I should like to draw attention to some aspects of Rogers' thinking. I purposefully emphasized above that to Rogers the relationship is of primary importance. What is more important for him than anything else is a warm attitude of acceptance on the part of the therapist—a complete acceptance of the other man, not only with his more particular sympathetic aspects, but with a great deal of unconditional positive regard which can very well be compared to love in the sense of the gospel love, as we have seen above. I believe that we can learn some very important things from Rogers for the carrying out of conversations with those in our pastoral care.

In the first place we can learn from him what "being beside the other man" is psychologically. We mentioned above that this was a condition *sine qua non* for a successful pastoral conversation. I believe, in fact, that this aspect is one of the greatest weaknesses in our pastoral work. In the analysis of pastoral conversations, which we will introduce in a more detailed fashion in the next chapter, it often becomes apparent that the education of a student to be a preacher, who is expected to know all the answers, who feels himself to be an expert, and who because of his position has a tendency to moralize and dogmatize, causes difficulties; precisely, being beside the other man, as we have seen in the case of the prophets and as Rogers has extensively analyzed, causes us trouble. The warm acceptance of another, seeing him always in the light of God's love, staying within his frame of reference, the habit of feeling and thinking with another and not listening in an authoritative way, the inner relaxation and freedom which are necessary for a good pastoral contact—all these factors indeed cause us very great difficulty in practice.

I think we must go so far as to state that the objections which Rogers has developed against a directive method of carrying out a conversation can free us pastors from a moralizing and authoritarian pastoral method and can show us the way to a real biblical type of pastoral guidance orientated on the great prophets and Christ himself. In a certain sense we could call Rogers' therapy a special method of pastoral care. He wants to help people come to stand in the light of an inwardly liberated life and is convinced that the power of a sincere, nonauthoritative love really can help them. Perhaps here we can speak—as with other psychotherapy— of a secularized form of pastoral care.

I want to follow up this theme and remark that the difference between Rogers and a pastor is that Rogers wants to help people help themselves, or perhaps more accurately, become themselves, while the pastor wants to help them find the right relationship with God or realize that they are standing in the light of God. In his work the pastor meets two problems. The first is that he does not see that many people who come to him with difficulties or with whose troubles he comes into contact have as the problem of their lives the lack of a right relationship with God because they have not sufficiently found themselves. If they are helped, wholly following the principles of Rogers, to talk about themselves, one then notices that they themselves find and accept the right relationship to God, so that we have nothing further to do but to listen and think with them. Indeed, they are helped by us to help themselves in problems such an inability to pray, rebellion against suffering, and the fear of doubt. So there is room for counseling in Rogers' sense in direct pastoral work, and every other approach to these problems would be directive in the wrong sense and therefore fly wide of the mark. Secondly, in order to preach in the pastoral meaning of the word we must be beside the other man in the most profound sense; that is to say, we must be there where the perspective of God in his existence becomes clearly visible, where, in other words, both pastor and parishioner can understand that he, the parishioner, is standing either within or outside the beam of God's love, where he is in a position to be called to belief. Here the metaphor of Fosdick's comes to mind: one may not land on an island before circumnavigating the whole and discovering the right landing place. We must be sure that we are not being directive in the wrong way and that what we are going to say will mean a real liberation, even though it will perhaps make things difficult for the other man.

Here we must mention something which is not discussed by Rogers and which gives the pastoral conversation its own dimension. When we help a person to discover himself, an integration will undoubtedly take place, a finding of the self in its most profound sense. But this finding of the self does not always mean a solution to the problems with which the person is struggling— sometimes only a reduction to, and intensification of, what seem to be the fundamental problems. I am thinking here of what Jaspers calls "border or frontier situations"—death, suffering, inner strife, and guilt. There are cases which, however often in practice they lie hidden under neurotic entanglements, are, in fact, normal conflicts of existence which cannot be healed by psychotherapy but can only be conquered by faith.

Therefore, it is possible that Rogers' type of psychotherapy can bring men to a real acceptance of their guilt toward neighbors and toward God. One thinks of the prodigal son who arrived at a deeper realization the hard way, something which we can compare to a psychotherapeutic result. In the darkness of such an existential situation the "preaching" of a pastor can bring a man to faith, that is to say, to a trusting surrender to God's love. Pastoral care to the sick is really always such a process, which technically formulated begins as psychotherapy and ends as pastoral care. It seems to me, therefore, that the American idea is right; that one must get clinical training in hospitals and psychiatric centers because there one develops the sensitivity which is a necessary condition of all pastoral care by meeting with people in stress situations, or as we would say, "frontier or border situations."

I think it is perfectly understandable that these problems are not dealt with within the framework of Rogers' work. He is a psychotherapist, and the people who go to him for advice do not expect religious answers from him; they see him in the role of counselor, not in that of spiritual adviser. It is also probable that people with religious problems would not go to him but rather to their minister; if they go to him they do so just because they do not want to be set in a religious dimension. The role that we play in other people's minds determines our relationship considerably, and fixes barriers so firmly that we cannot step over them. Thus, if Rogers did reveal his beliefs in such a situation, he would do so as a fellow believer and not as a psychotherapist. Of course, it is not impossible to step outside one's role; there are doctors who in certain circumstances throw off their role of being doctors and talk to their patients as fellow believers—a gesture which in these circumstances can be a blessing to the patient, but it can also be undesirable, particularly in a psychotherapist. Perhaps I can add here that, of course, we as pastors also fill a predetermined role in the eyes of those with whom we come in contact. This means that the other man approaches us with definite expectations. Thus it can be a disappointment to him if at a certain moment we do not play our part as he expected it whatever the reason and, for example, do not say a prayer. A clear understanding of our role, of our task as pastors, is necessary for every conversation in which we take part plus an image of that role which the other man expects from us—and perhaps even fears. I would add here that circumstances can arise in which the pastor has to ask himself whether he can go through with the part he is expected to play. He would have to face this question if in a certain context he were asked to do something in a superstitious way, such as offering a prayer for rain. However, it can lie deeper and be more difficult than this. As pastor I once had to disappoint someone by saying that what he really needed was psychotherapeutic treatment and that he had really come to me in order to get out of making this decision. I can think of certain habits which as minister one has no right to sanction by advising prayer or turning to the gospel; though on the other hand, the person concerned must not get the idea that we are not standing by him entirely.

We have, however, wandered rather far from the point. What I want to make plain here is that the pastoral conversation's own dimension does not come to the fore explicitly in the psychotherapeutic field, although it can be seen in the frontier cases. Here the psychotherapist will retire as psychotherapist and let the client find his own way in the light of his own tradition (up-bringing, social milieu, etc.). By now he is adult, and the psychotherapist's job ends the far side of his infantile, neurotic conflicts. To complete this picture perhaps we should remark that in many cases psychotherapeutic treatment does have a concealed religious aspect implicit in it. The process of the client coming to himself can be experienced as a religious experience by both client and psychotherapist. We meet here a type of religious humanism such as is defended by someone like Erich Fromm in his *Psychoanalysis and Religion*, and which I think is accepted by many psychotherapists and plays a much more important part in the thinking of doctors than is generally realized. It is a type of religion that gives a different message to that of Christendom at just those moments which Jaspers calls frontier situations. Jaspers is himself a noble example of this type of religion.

The second thing which we pastors can learn from Rogers is how standing beside another can deepen into standing beside him in the fundamental decisions of his life. Rogers' experience is that through the relief given by positive regard a dynamic process begins in the client, by which he comes to himself in the deepest sense of the word.

In the Rogers quotation given previously we can see how this process generally develops. The empathic reflection, or, if we do not want to put too much emphasis on the technical side of the relationship (for Rogers the technique of a conversation is only a useful means to an end), the careful sharing of feelings and thoughts which the client brings with him, is taken so far that the many decisions which he has to take in his life can be done adequately because he has become congruent with the deepest strivings in himself. Rogers' term "congruent" means, he says, the same as "integrated," "sincere," "authentic." In other words, the man now lives, as it were, out of a fundamental decision in which he has accepted himself as he really is, so that from now on he behaves in line with this acceptance; he is no longer motivated neurotically from fear or desire to maintain his own position aided by all sorts of defense mechanisms, but he is instead relaxed and, in the real sense of the word, objective. In Jaspers' terminology—it is a pity that it is almost unknown in America—we could say that the person is now "himself in freedom." Of course, this is the ideal result of psychotherapy; in truth no one can completely attain this goal.

Thinking along Rogers' lines, we can now formulate faith as

the acceptance of oneself as standing in God's light, and pastoral care in this way becomes a question of being in communication with the other man in such a way that he can make this decision of faith. Two things are necessary here: first, indicating the perspective toward God, the prophetic witness; and then, being so close beside the other man that a spark can fly across so that the *testimonium spiritus sancti* as we have seen above can do illuminating and liberating work. We do not sufficiently know the psychological process that takes place here and the conditions for this process, and I am convinced that a closer study of the well-known phenomenon of identification in psychoanalysis can bring us further here.

Once again I should like to return to Fosdick's metaphor of sailing round an island. It becomes clear from a closer analysis of the dynamic process in the other person that one can and may only begin to talk of real pastoral care when the process of becoming oneself or accepting oneself is completed, in other words, when the pastor has accompanied the other man well on his way there. If the pastor turns too soon to what he thinks is pastoral care, then it appears that he is moralizing and dogmatizing instead of witnessing and is directive in the wrong sense. It is clear that the great importance of Rogers for our pastoral work is that he sharpens our self-criticism and makes us conscious that in general we are too quick to preach and admonish. The great worth of clinical training consists not so much in the formal knowledge that one acquires there as in this use of self-criticism in the getting accustomed to an attitude of cautious, thoughtful, and loving thinking and feeling with the other man, which rises from the deepest wells of the gospel message, and in being prepared to accompany him to that point in his life where he is clearly able to see that he is standing on the dividing line between light and darkness. Clinical training teaches the pastor to listen to himself and to the other person and to both

combined in such a way that listening to God comes almost un-
bidden. We return now for a moment to the beginning of Chapter
1 where the suggestion was made that a conversation—and certainly a pastoral one—is a dynamic process. I hope that the most
important aspects of this process have become a good deal clearer
now. We could schematically state that a pastoral conversation
runs its course in two stages. One of a more or less lengthy duration
in which the pastor by his empathic thinking helps the other person come to an understanding of the fundamental decision which
confronts him in this present situation. In the other, shorter
stage the perspective of God then opens up before him. The pastor
indicates to the other person, in words that can be understood and
in a tone fitting to this communication, the light in which the
person stands and which he has not yet or has but insufficiently seen.
When I reflect on the examples given above, it seems to me that the
qualities that the pastor needs more than anything else are humility,
stamina, obedience, and love.

There is a third point that we can learn from Rogers for the
carrying out of a conversation. It is a point that we have not yet
definitely discussed but which lies hidden implicit in the whole
argument; that the psychotherapist (and the pastor) must himself
be well integrated in his contact with other people. We can define
this more simply by saying that he must be inwardly free and relaxed in his relationship to his opposite number in a conversation.
Perhaps he too has personal problems, but these must not stop him
from being completely at the other man's disposal. He must also be
sufficiently relaxed so that he does not repress certain feelings of
uncertainty or worry which he feels rising in him during a conversation, in this way erecting an artificial facade with which to confront the other man. Instead, he must dare to acknowledge these to
himself and so let them come up into his consciousness, which, of

course, does not mean to say that he should share his feelings with the other person during a conversation. However, he must be aware of them in such a way that he is not afraid to speak about them to someone else, for example, a supervisor. One can indeed state that one of the advantages of working under supervision, and thus one of the advantages of clinical training, is that one is less tied to these feelings of uncertainty which may arise during the course of a conversation and so can better maintain the integrity of that conversation.

For pastors particularly it is wise to follow Rogers' warning to beware of talking about our own personal lives during a pastoral conversation. It can be a relief for someone else to experience that he is not the only one to suffer certain difficulties and that we too face them in our lives. If, however, that which we divulge to him is such that he then loses his feeling of security in our integrity, because we who should be lovingly at his service expose our uncertainty to him, then the possibility of pastoral care has been destroyed. The story goes that Luther was once visited by a young colleague who told him that he had such difficulties with preaching the gospel that often on Saturdays he did not know whether he would be in a proper state to preach on Sunday. Luther is said to have looked at him and answered, "You too, brother?" It would have been depressing rather than relieving had he answered, "I have just been talking to a colleague about this very problem because I too am worried by it, but I don't seem to be making much headway."

I hope it has become clear that Rogers' "method" can open our eyes to important aspects of pastoral conversation, which, though we have vaguely sensed them ourselves, we have not satisfactorily been able to disentangle and formulate. It is time to return to the reality of a pastoral conversation.

III

Starting the Pastoral Conversation

In this chapter I want to make a preliminary reconnaissance in the field of conversation analysis. Without getting too involved in technical details or bothering ourselves with special terms and formulas, I want to take a look at a conversation between an untrained minister and one of his parishioners, the sort of talk a person carries out daily.

It is a conversation with a woman who has rung up and asked for an appointment. On entering she is obviously nervous. The minister knows her as a regular churchgoer. She is the mother of four children, and, seen from the outside, her family is a perfectly ordinary one. Neither husband nor wife are on intimate terms with the minister. The woman comes into the study and says, "I hope I'm not troubling you, Vicar. I know you're very busy."

Those who have taken part in the exercise of finding, at conversation analysis seminars, the right answer to a similar opening sentence in a talk know how particularly helpful it is to discuss together in a group the different possibilities open to the minister. Obviously we cannot imitate this method here in this book. I can only suggest that the reader take the trouble to do for himself what the participants in the exercise were expected to do, namely, to write two sentences (complete sentences!) on a piece of paper— one sentence which the minister ought not to have answered and one which he might well have used. It is even instructive to note down at the same time why we think one to be the right answer and the other wrong.

I shall now discuss some of the possible answers which could be made. The reader can then check for himself what he makes of his written answers in the light of my remarks. It is probable that he will feel compelled to revise his opinions. Perhaps we will be in agreement, but it is also likely that the reader will not agree with me and will want to stick to his original opinions. In a certain sense I hope that this will be the case with those reading this book. Its intention is not to attempt to force a certain interpretation of pastoral conversations onto the reader, but rather to set him thinking, to arouse doubts, and to spur him on to some critical considerations. In this way he will come, I hope, to a style of pastoral work, a working attitude as it were, which in the good sense of the word is pastoral and yet is at the same time thoroughly personal and real. In the coming pages of this book I shall more than once take the opportunity to explain what I mean by this.

The First Responses

I will repeat the sentence: "I hope that I'm not troubling you, Vicar. I know you're very busy." To begin with—what must the minister *not* say? I will give a few examples of the wrong answer with arguments to show why I think they are wrong. I believe that this first answer will not raise much disagreement among readers.

a. "Yes, I am pretty busy, but please sit down."

At the very best we can hope that the minister here is at least telling the truth. But even if that were so he ought not to say so. Why? It is not very easy to put in words, but anyone can feel that such an answer would fail to create the right atmosphere for a more or less confidential conversation. The minister must not say that the caller is a trouble or say that he has not much time. Not merely because there was an appointment made previously by telephone to which the woman could refer, but far more because the woman ought to be able to rely on a readiness to be interested and sympathetic on the minister's part. That is what he is a minister for. Anyone who listens well can hear in the woman's words the expression, "I hope you have time and interest for me," and such an answer as this from the minister would put an end to this hope and make it extremely difficult for her to continue unconcernedly.

b. "I seem to be a bad minister; I hear this remark once or twice practically every day."

The minister here is obviously nettled. Here, too, the right atmosphere for a pastoral conversation cannot be created. He has not grasped that the woman said what she did from uncertainty and gives his own feelings free rein. There is no sympathetic contact. In fact, the woman will probably think she has not been understood and, indeed, feel misunderstood.

c. "Don't let's beat about the bush too long. You made an appointment by telephone; what's troubling you?"

Even if this answer were not given in a gruff tone of voice but in a businesslike way—an argument which some people could perhaps bring in favor of this being a fitting reply—I would still consider it impossible. The woman's words clearly reveal her hesitant approach; something is bothering her which she is not going to find easy to talk about. She would feel cold-shouldered by this answer. It seems as if the minister cannot imagine that another person might dread having to talk.

I would hammer home once more how obvious these opening sentences—and, indeed, how often does a talk begin this way?— make the thesis that it is not the exchange of words but the feelings which determine the shape of the conversation. This consideration must help us when searching for the right answers.

We begin by supposing that the woman exposes by her words one or more lively but varying emotions. She is uncertain of herself; she is frightened that the minister will not have time for her— that is to say, no interest in her. Apparently she feels that what she wants to say is not going to be easy to talk about. For her it is something very important, but what will the minister think of it? By telephoning and making an appointment she has a certain claim to the minister's time, but seeing what she has to talk about, was that justifiable? The minister must give her an answer in which she feels that he understands what is going on in her and that at the same time he does not mind. He must not cold-shoulder her nor more or less openly ignore her feelings, but he should say something in which she gets the feeling that he is trying to make contact with her, that he is with her in the literal meaning of the words. A too simple, businesslike answer is thus not sufficient. There must be a certain feeling of sympathy. An answer such as "It's no trouble, and since you made the appointment I've kept time for you" still remains too aloof and is therefore insufficiently pastoral.

I should like to give you some possible answers to consider.

a. "You don't like trespassing on a parson's time."

b. "You find it rather difficult to take your questions to someone whom you think is so busy."

c. "I have kept this hour free, so I hope we'll have time for a good talk together."

I shall admit straight away to preferring *a.* or *b.* Later on I hope to make it clear why this is so. I must also add that I expect all these answers to be given in a calm, understanding tone of voice. It is only when one begins to speak in a different tone that one realizes what a great role feelings play in human contacts. One can utter words in such a way that the conversant gets the impression that his feelings are quite ignored.

The conversation continues, and the woman says, "I have such a difficult problem I hardly know how to talk about it," and lapses into silence. What ought the minister to say now and what not? We shall continue our investigation as we did with the first sentence. Once again I expect the reader to write down two sentences, the right and the wrong answer with, if necessary, an explanation for them.

In my opinion the following answers would be wrong:

a. "My experience is that once you start talking about something it's generally easier than you think. I suggest you just begin."

On first sight this is the most obvious answer for a minister to make. However, I do not believe it to be the right one. It seems as if the minister is doing his best to help the other person in her uncertainty—and in his own eyes he is doing this—but in fact he is not standing beside her. This is really an attempt to force a situation which threatens to stick fast into motion by not taking the other person's scruples seriously. The woman will then feel this as a lack of understanding of her difficulties and will have real trouble in explaining what is worrying her. Or perhaps she will take the plunge with the courage of despair, but this is not a good way to begin a worthwhile conversation. I could even imagine that certain very sensitive people would simply jump up and say: "No, Vicar, I can't! I'm sorry to have bothered you."

b. "May I ask if it has something to do with the children?"

Because the woman remains silent the minister has to take the initiative and make a move. This situation can indeed be compared to a game of chess. It is understandable that he tries to find out something about her difficulties and so asks a question. Obviously, there is every sort of trouble that she could be in and which she wants to divulge to the minister: her marriage, problems with her husband, perhaps something she has done wrong herself, or something in connection with the children—dishonesty, bad school reports, the need to find a temporary home for one of them for some reason or other. But it can also be something of a quite different nature: a talk with the doctor who had to tell her that something serious was wrong, a threatening operation which she cannot face up to and which, in fact, is shattering her whole faith.

I imagine that the minister has intuitively felt along these lines in the few seconds that have passed and in order not to unbalance her more chooses the seemingly most innocent subject to get her to start talking. But does it in fact really help the woman in this way? Perhaps it does concern the children—particularly if it is not anything particularly serious to do with them—but if it concerns her husband or fear that she has cancer, or if one of the children has done something really serious, stolen something or the like, what then? Then the minister's question will not get him any further, because whatever it is that bars her from unburdening herself has not been removed. On the contrary, by now she must more or less have the feeling "the minister doesn't really understand me; he doesn't expect me to talk about that terrible thing I have to say. Is he, with his happy marriage and normal children, really the man who could understand me?" She may not be conscious of so strong a reaction as I have expressed, yet I am sure that the putting of such a question would induce similar feelings of disappointment in her. It is always useful to put oneself in another's shoes, and if I do this here, I sense something of her disappointment arising in me.

At this stage in the analysis of the progress of a conversation, I expect a more or less negative response from the reader. He probably starts by asking: "What is the point of all this? Is it possible to carry out a conversation in this way? What has happened to intuition that tells one at a certain moment what to say and what not to say? And aren't we underestimating here the tone of voice in which something is said? Doesn't the tone of voice create the atmosphere through which our real meaning becomes clear?"

I would certainly cheer such a reaction. Because only when we can express this sort of criticism and discuss together do we really get any further. Book form is a very defective way for reaching positive results in this field. A live discussion in which word and counter-word have their place is much more productive. This is one of the great advantages of clinical training. In extensive group or individual discussions there is plenty of time to take up these points and in mutual thought and argument arrive at a common opinion. In one way I consider the usefulness of this book to lie in the making of its readers conscious of the worth of clinical training.

Now let me say two things about the questions formulated above. In the first place, I entirely agree that in an actual conversation the considerations which up till now have been so minutely discussed would not play much of a role. It would make the development of a conversation completely impossible if the minister had to be aware of all these things every time the other person opened his mouth. Of course, he must use his intuition for all it is worth. I see in this objection only support for my thesis that a conversation is more than just an exchange of words, and that when man attempts to communicate with his fellows his feelings play a determining role. I should consider it an important step forward in our appreciation of these problems if for the rest of this book we agree that we start from this point of view.

Secondly, I hope that as this book unfolds it will become clear that the word "intuition" does not cover everything. I personally believe that we must trust not only in our intuition, but in our pastoral attitude, which in turn sharpens, as it were, our intuition which has continued to work all the time. From the analysis of conversations—later on in this book we shall attempt to analyze reports of real conversations—it turns out that our great difficulty is that we react too fast, in other words, that our real appreciation of the conversation works too slowly, or is not sufficiently acute. One can also express it thus: our pastoral attitude is not enough our inner possession. We have too little understanding of the role we must play in the conversation; we do not sufficiently act from the standpoint of being a pastor. In this book I hope to be able to give more meaning to these somewhat vague phrases.

Establishing a Sense of Acceptance

But now let us return to our conversation. The woman has said: "I have such a difficult problem I hardly know how to talk about it," and has lapsed into silence. What should the minister do now? It is obvious enough that his only task is to set the woman at ease so that she can unburden herself. It will not help to understate the difficulties in one way or another; on the contrary, it will make things more difficult. This is so in both following instances:

a. when the difficulty rests in finding the right words to express herself if she is an uneducated sort of person (in the case of a businessman's wife that would hardly be the case).

b. when there is within her a resistance which hinders her desire to lay her troubles bare.

One could suppose that the minister could remain silent in an understanding way and wait calmly for her to speak. Such a silence is indeed a positive answer, and the fear that so many people have of a pause in the conversation is often wrong. Being silent and listening to the silence can help the other person. But here right at the beginning of the talk the chance of such a silence being embarrassing seems considerable, and I think it is the minister's job here to find a few words to help the woman on.

In fact, I can only think of one sentence which he could use: "You find it difficult to tell me." The choice of words and phraseology could of course be different, but the meaning should be this, and it should be said in such a way that the woman senses that the minister is in sympathy with her. I ought perhaps to give here my reasons for thinking this, but I have reserved it for the following chapter where I have dealt with it in detail. However, I will just point out here that the woman is in need of but one thing, namely, the assurance that in her hesitation the minister understands and accepts her for what she is. She is waiting until the atmosphere is that in which she can confide certain very confidential and intimate things. Thus, by such a phrase as this the minister shows that he understands what is going on in her and that he does not want to force the pace, and so he creates the right atmosphere. Once we grasp this point we can understand why it is the prime concern of Carl Rogers, whose ideas about conversing were discussed in the last chapter.

Now to continue with what the woman then says in her third sentence. After the minister has spoken, she says in a rather offhand manner: "I've discovered that my husband has been having an affair with his secretary for the last two years." Then she suddenly bursts into a storm of tears: "What do you think of that?"

So here again what must the minister definitely not say, and what ought he to say? The minister must not say:

a. "When did you discover this?"

The not asking of this question undoubtedly adds to the minister's difficulties. He must, if he is going to help or advise, know some facts of the case. But at this moment the question is misplaced. The woman is not yet ready for this sort of fact-finding question; she is obviously overburdened with all kinds of bottled-up emotions. Some way or another these must be dealt with first. The minister may be aware that he has asked this question at this point chiefly because he fears a continuation of the conversation in which all sorts of uncontrolled emotions may be let loose. He feels somewhat uneasy and would rather turn the conversation into another direction.

Here we have hit upon a problem which in a certain sense is itself a pastoral question. In such a conversation are the clergy sometimes uncertain or anxious, or perhaps even aggressive?

If this is so, why are they? Or, more important, is this permissible? What should we do about it?

This is not really the place to discuss this—further on in this book the problem will be discussed in detail—but perhaps I should point out here that the minister himself often is not aware that he is conversing under the influence of lively emotions of uncertainty or resentment. Witness the minister quoted in the first chapter. But the other partner in the conversation—here the woman—may well notice it, even if she cannot define what it is that irritates her in the minister's words. We could express it thus: she expresses very clearly in her words a strong emotion—or rather, combination of emotions—and by this response the minister ignores them. The result is that she feels she is not understood and even that, in a sense, she is being kept at a distance. She will need time to recover from this disappointment and will remain afraid to speak about her feelings in a natural way, or, shall we say, to expose these emotions.

Perhaps I should note here that after a moment's silence in which the woman has time to control herself, the minister could say "When did you find out?" in a soft, sympathetic voice, hereby inviting her in an understanding way to continue her story. Then, of course, the objections cited above are less valid. Yet I can still think of a happier reaction to the woman's revelation.

b. "Oh, how terrible!"

These words, which coming from a good friend of her own sex would probably be well placed, are inept for the carrying out of a pastoral conversation. I see it so. By these words the minister joins forces with the woman but does not stand next to or beside her. These words express no feeling of understanding or support for the woman. They are an exclamation and really add nothing to the conversation. In addition, the minister is not sufficiently impartial or at a distance—a distance which, in spite of his sympathy, he must retain.

c. "This is very wrong."

The minister here answers the question put to him by the woman. He gives his opinion of unfaithfulness in marriage, a judgment which to him is always valid and therefore can be made here, too. Everyone, a minister also, has the tendency to think in terms of black or white. A person's opinion is asked and he gives it, but without keeping in mind the actual people whom the question concerns. Am I very far out when I remark that this straightforward type of thinking is one of the great obstacles in the pastoral cure of souls where we are always dealing primarily with people; and where we can deal adequately with their struggle to keep to the right standards and commandments only within that larger context? We need not lose sight of the sacredness of these standards and commandments (Is not the story in John 8:1-11 concerning the adulterous woman always a sublime example for us?) if we always see them in connection to the actual people who are involved. So long as a minister says in this emphatic way: "This is very wrong," he is, as far as I am concerned, still standing in the shoes of the scribes and Pharisees who brought the woman to Jesus. They, too, only considered the breaking of the commandment and not the actual person whom she was or they were.

But apart from this, such an answer is particularly dangerous for the further good development of the conversation. The minister has chosen sides in this conflict between husband and wife. The woman's question is really a sort of trap; she needs help against her husband from someone who believes she has the right on her side. Perhaps her sorrow is genuine, and the husband has behaved rottenly. But what if this is a case where the woman is really the guilty party, who, by her behavior has driven her husband into the arms of another woman, and who perhaps is herself beset with every kind of guilt feeling? It could be that the woman wants to set her own feelings at rest by hearing from the minister that her husband is indeed the guilty party; she may not even be conscious of this when she fires off her question at him. But however this may be, in giving his opinion thus the minister cuts off every chance of doing pastoral work for the good of everyone involved in this human problem. He has taken sides himself.

Further, by this answer he also cuts off any possibility of continuing the conversation in such a way that the woman comes to a more profound understanding of herself and perhaps even gains an insight into those of her own faults which have played a part in her present predicament. He fixes her attitude in her first aggressive reaction to the discovery. Experience shows that if a conversation gives the opportunity for every emotion—even repressed ones—to be expressed, a person can come to a more profound self-understanding, and the pastor himself will see much more clearly at what point in the life of this individual he ought to attempt to offer spiritual advice. Time and again it can be seen that not only for the clergy but for everyone committed to the help of their fellow man, it is a difficult lesson to learn not to have prepackaged advice or judgments ready to be handed out, but rather to let the other person talk himself completely out.

It is possible to think of more wrong answers. It makes a useful exercise and one which we regularly use in our clinical training sessions, where we search for as many examples as we can find and then try to prove to ourselves just why they are wrong.

Preserving the Pastoral Attitude

But now I will try to find the right answer. What line should we take when faced with such a situation in which we clearly see there are certain things we must not do? We cannot draw up a list of possibilities—we simply do not have the opportunity—and then quietly choose the one that probably fits the situation best. Here we come up against the problem of the pastoral attitude which we have met earlier and which will be discussed further in this book. We must be conscious of a certain role, a certain task, and must act from this realization. Thus it is not so much a question of the words we use—though these of course are not unimportant—but whether we have the right feelings toward our conversational partner with all his problems and whether the right words arise, as it were, unasked from this position.

As is so often said nowadays, we must stand in the right relationship with the other person guided by this fundamental attitude. We must literally want to stand beside him and in our own way be a pastor to him. Later on we shall go into this more extensively but perhaps one or two necessary qualities should be mentioned here: real interest and love, no desire to command him or find fault with him, respect for his freedom and own responsibility, and tolerance for those things which we ourselves find unsympathetic.

So in this case I would look for an answer in this direction. This woman after some hesitation reveals—however it may later on turn out and whatever role she may herself have played in this marriage drama—a great trouble. From her question it is clear that she is seeking the minister's support. Thus what she needs is indeed this support. As we have seen above, this must not be the support of having taken sides, but it certainly should be the support of someone who is sympathetic toward her, and who, if she wants it, is willing to try to find a solution. I would suggest that the minister say something like this:

a. "You are dreadfully shocked by this discovery, aren't you?"
b. "You feel, don't you, that you are faced with a situation which is almost overwhelming you?"

And now to the last sentence we shall tackle of this conversation. The woman says furiously: "It's all the fault of that little devil!" What must the minister not say?

a. "Yes, it often happens between the boss and his secretary at an office."

Anyone carefully reconsidering any of his own past talks with parishioners will often catch himself out holding up a conversation again and again by making a similar generalized remark. We must clearly understand how much we brake the other person's flow of feelings, if we may use this phrase, with such a remark. The ground on which this conversation up till now had been based and which had given it a certain framework, direction, and depth is by such a remark needlessly enlarged, immediately causing the direction and form of the conversation to vanish—and even making the other person feel neither entirely understood nor that the minister is at one with him. This is also the case in remarks such as: "People are dreadfully wicked nowadays," or "In just such a way can a marriage crisis arise."

b. "Have you actually asked yourself if you haven't been deficient in your relationship to your husband?"

It is clear enough what the minister means by this question or a similar one, which taken alone (see above) is understandable enough. But he is not only asking for information so that he can

63

re-create a clear picture of what has happened, but in order to moralize. The time is not yet ripe for this question; the woman has obviously much more to say and has certainly not unburdened herself of everything that is upsetting her emotionally. From the not incorrect point of view that it takes two to pick a quarrel, he has tried to bring the woman to some sort of admittance of guilt.

There are two things I should like to remark on here. Firstly, in a really good pastoral conversation the other person will at a certain point need to ask himself how much the present situation is a result of his own faults. It also seems that in general people learn far more from what they themselves have discovered in their confidential talks with us than from that which we tell or ask them. Secondly, moralizing means that we immediately stand in opposition to someone and so lose the contact of togetherness, of really standing beside the other. Indeed, we even appear to threaten the other man. He then reacts generally in an only partially positive way with, for example, such answers as "Yes, perhaps there's some right in what you say," or "Of course it takes two to make a quarrel, but . . ."; or, definitely negative, "But Vicar, you don't understand." The other person feels himself set aside and misunderstood by our moralizing.

What then ought the minister to do?

In my opinion not much more than attempt to feel and think with the woman and in this way give her the opportunity to really say everything she wants to. The flow of feelings must not be dammed up but by our standing by be given the opportunity of finding its right outlet. We should pass no judgment either for or against, ignore nothing but consider what she wants to express, and by repeating in our words what she is expressing in her feelings, give her a clear picture of what she is driving at. My suggestion would be to say: "You have the feeling that the secretary is at the bottom of all this." The woman can then go on in any direction which is important for her—sketch in the role of the secretary, give an account of the part taken by the husband, etc.

There is no need to pursue the start of the pastoral conversation any further. It is time to turn our attention to some of its other aspects. But enough has been said to make it plain that Rogers' ideas can serve us well as a working hypothesis, however much we may wish to call on others as well. It must be clear that the direction of a conversation—and thus also the success or failure of it—is largely determined by feelings. It is a dynamic, and not merely a logical, process.

IV

Principle and Process
in Pastoral Conversation

In this chapter I want to try to get deeper into the pastoral conversation. We are dealing with a dynamic encounter which cannot be adequately described by enumerating principles. It is also a process which must be analyzed. We take the conversation in which a hospital chaplain, who when visiting a ward and going from bed to bed without knowing much about the patients lying there, finds a woman whom he has never visited before. She has apparently just been admitted for an operation. Ministers often have this sort of contact in their study or when paying calls, so every minister can draw useful conclusions for his own work from this conversation. We have also chosen a hospital setting because, as we have seen, we can learn much for more normal conversations from conversations with people in stress-situations; the important elements of pastoral care generally come out more clearly in these.

The minister goes up to the bed and introduces himself. He explains that he is the hospital chaplain, asks the woman where she comes from and other information and inquires about her illness. Then in order to give the conversation a more definite shape and not lose too much time with details which are beside the point, he says: "Is there anything you'd like me to do for you?" We imagine that, because of the relationship which has meanwhile been established, this is the best way of saying what he wants to express. In other cases a different formula would be more fitting.

The sick woman, somewhat unsure of herself and worried, replies: "I would so like you to pray with me."

We shall go to work here much as we did in Chapter 3 and ask ourselves what the minister ought to answer and what he must not answer. Once again it will probably be a good idea if the reader first writes down two verbatim answers—one the right, and the other the wrong answer—with, if possible, the motives lying behind these answers. I shall do the same and hope that the reader will join me in an imaginary discussion. Simply because a conversation is a dynamic process in which feelings play a great part, it always consists of something creative that cannot be rationalized completely, which has its own individual coloring and opportune development. In this sort of analysis, therefore, I do not intend to provide definite recipes but to sharpen our intuition. This occurs best when we exchange opinions by word and counter-word. Particularly after the last chapter the lines on which a pastoral conversation ought to run should have become clear. How these lines are followed in practice always remains a discovery of the moment, demanding a touch of artistry.

In this chapter, however, I want to reverse the pattern of Chapter 3, first discussing what the minister should answer and after that what he should not. It seems to me that at this moment this alteration is better pedagogically speaking.

Keeping the Focus on Feelings

To recapitulate: After some introductory remarks and the offer from the minister to do something for the sick woman, she says hesitantly and in a worried way, "I would so like you to pray with me." We have learned that the attitude of the pastor must be directed toward the feelings expressed in the words spoken by the other person. In this case this is particularly difficult because the woman makes a definite request, one which a minister often hears and to which he almost always reacts positively. Here he can hardly answer on the content of her question, for the conversation is not far enough advanced for him to know what thought he should express in his prayer; is she experiencing difficulties with her faith, is she feeling guilty about something, is she afraid, and if so, why? The request has an objective content but clearly expresses an emotion—we can hear it in her voice and see it in her face. Something such as: "I need you, I need prayer, I can't find the answer." In this case the feelings are the most important element. The minister, should he react only to the content of the question, will inevitably ignore the emotion behind it, and the woman will feel that she is not entirely understood or accepted. The conversation would undoubtedly suffer from this. So I suggest that the minister could say.

"You have the feeling that I could help you if I spoke about your difficulties to God."

The choice of words could be different, but this formulation is made in an attempt to remain within the frame of reference of this woman; the minister had offered to do something for her, and she, speaking hesitatingly and fearfully (thus from a definite problem) has asked him to pray with her. What the minister then does is to reflect the feeling which he has sensed in the woman back to her. This will awake the feelings in her that the minister understands her, accepts her in her uncertainty, and so stands next to her. In particular, a sympathetic tone of voice is an important factor here. By speaking these words the minister approaches the woman in a friendly and sympathetic way, not as a threatening nor as a censorious figure but as a man who gives a feeling of safety, to whom it is possible to talk one's heart out, and so the woman goes on and explains why she has made this request. The minister's words are more or less an invitation to continue.

It is not difficult to report a number of reactions on the part of the minister which could at this stage of the talk disturb its course, although they are well meant.

I mention the following:

a. "I should like to do that, just tell me what we are to pray about."

This is the answer which, as I mentioned above, by reacting on the content and not on the feelings behind it, damns up the flow of feeling and chills the conversation. One can understand this best by putting oneself in the woman's position for a moment.

b. "It is sometimes difficult to find the right words for a prayer."

The minister here senses that in this case it is no use just folding his hands and saying a prayer, and he tries to say something to help the woman. But he begins to generalize and so diverts the conversation from that which must stand centrally—the feeling of uncertainty and fear in the woman herself.

c. "You've been lying there fretting."

This is interpretation and diagnosis. In a way this does help because it makes it clear to the woman that the pastor is engrossed in her problem and sympathizes with her, but she also gets the feeling that he is sitting at a distance observing her. He is not standing next to her but keeping too great a distance. Thus this answer does not help to further the conversation. Whatever could the woman say now? If she has difficulties about which she scarcely dares to speak, this answer, unless given in a very fatherly tone of voice— and this may be dangerous, too—does not create the right atmosphere in which the woman would feel confident enough to go on.

d. "It is a pity that we do not learn to pray when we are fit; now just when we need to we cannot."

This is moralizing. The minister, perhaps well-meaningly, wants to offer moral advice; the woman ought to resolve to learn to pray in normal conditions. What he actually does is to disappear outside the woman's frame of reference, leaving her still burdened with her feelings of fear and uncertainty. Not only is she given a lecture which, if it is to be accepted, presupposes a good relationship, but she is also made to feel an outcast, rejected. Thus, by so moralizing a serious break is made in the relationship while the flow of feelings is shattered. After such a remark it is practically impossible to get the conversation back onto the right rails.

e. "Prayer is a good support for faith in difficult situations."

This is dogmatizing. One could also call it generalizing. The minister—probably as well-meaning as the last—wants to get over to the woman how pleased he is with her request. But simply because of this he separates himself from the woman. He is not thinking of her and her troubles any more but of himself and his dogmatic approach to prayer. The woman's interest which is centered on her difficulties, and considering her circumstances rightly so, is more or less violently pulled away and fixed onto a private idea of the minister's. The flow of feelings is broken, and this must give rise to mild irritation in the woman if not to a sense of disappointment.

So much for the reaction of the minister to the woman's first request. We continue now with the conversation. We must suppose that the minister has said something to the effect that "You have the feeling that I could help you if we prayed together"—just as in the suggestion given above he tries to remain within the frame of reference of the patient. The woman appears to feel secure in the atmosphere of the relationship which is developing here and says: "I'm going to be operated on tomorrow, and I can't face it."

Now what ought the minister to say, and what must he refrain from saying? My suggestion is that once again he should sympathetically reflect the feelings that the statement cloak. For instance he could answer:

"You have the feeling that this operation is approaching you as something threatening?"

or if one considers the opening phrase "you have the feeling" too formal,

"You find it awfully difficult to realize that you are going to be operated on tomorrow."

If these words of the minister are just read, it seems that he does nothing and so adds nothing to the conversation. Is not what is developing here just turning into a dead game of ping-pong? I can only state that the proof of the pudding is in the eating. Ministers who have had the courage to make clear to others in this way in a pastoral conversation that they were interested in the expression of the others' feelings, and that they are doing their best to be with the others, have discovered how in this way their contacts have become steadily deeper and more personal. This active listening—as it can perhaps best be called—creates a particularly fruitful and trustful relationship. This can be seen from what follows here.

Avoid Tempting Sidetracks

I will not repeat what I have already said above about what takes place in the other person when a minister reacts in this way. I only want to indicate briefly the hidden "tempting" sidetracks that open up before the pastor at such a point in the conversation and which he must avoid.

Sidetracks which in one way or another will bring a conversation to a dead end are, for example:

a. Seizing the content and ignoring the feelings:
   "Let us bring this problem before God in a prayer."

The minister is convinced that he now knows what the reason is for the woman's uncertainty and turns to deal with it. But is he really so sure? Has he circumnavigated the island? Is it outside the bounds of possibility that the woman still does not feel fully understood and therefore also rejected?

b. Moralizing and so rejecting the woman's feelings or anyway belittling them:
   "Nowadays doctors are so able you mustn't let yourself get so upset."

c. Generalizing and so disturbing the flow of feelings:
   "Many people can't face up to an operation, even if it isn't an important one."

72

d. Diagnostic:
"Apparently you find it difficult to accept your lot."

e. Interpretive:
"Such fears sometimes depend on very early childhood memories."

In these last two answers the patient has become an object of psychological analysis and so will get the feeling that we are not standing next to her. In neither case has the feeling that the patient has expressed been followed up, and the minister is outside her frame of reference.

We continue now on the basis of the suggested right answer, and in the thus deepened relationship—for the woman has found in the pastor a sympathetic, careful listener—she says: "I'm so ashamed that I don't have enough faith."

I can imagine that at this point some of my readers are getting more or less impatient with the passive attitude of the pastor, an attitude which on paper does seem rather ridiculous. I imagine them feeling: "But now we are clearly treading on pastoral ground; we really do not need to continue with this silly parrotlike game." All I can say is that I sympathize with this reaction. I too have felt impatience rising in me during many a conversation analysis. But I do ask that my argument be followed. I am convinced that the hidden persuader at this point in a conversation is the almost vocal invitation to the preacher or theologian in us to step in; not to mince my words, to be in Carl Rogers' terminology "directive"; not, and this is my greatest objection, in the deepest sense which we have agreed in the earlier chapters, to be essential in all real pastoral care, but in the more superficial sense of "helping the other person quickly in the right direction." This is not only not circumnavigating the island but also not leaving the other man to

73

take the real responsibility for his own life and decisions, which remains a fundamental principle for real pastoral care.

I suggest here that once again the feelings of this woman ought to be reflected as best, closely, and lovingly possible. I do not need to repeat the reasons for this: So the minister might then say:

"You blame yourself that now, so to speak, your faith has let you down."

What are the side tracks a minister should avoid?

a. The soothing generalization:
"You are not alone in this; there are few people in such a situation as this who would dare to say that they have enough belief. Think for a moment of Christ in Gethsemane."

b. The well-meaning belittling:
"But in the circumstances there's nothing wrong in recognizing a moment of doubt."

c. Making the case interesting by dogmatizing:
"You mustn't forget that in Gethsemane Christ also asked that the cup be taken from him."

d. The fatherly moralization:
"I can think of worse things than a moment's doubt before an operation."

Of course there are more, but one thing they all have in common is that the feeling which the patient shows is not altogether taken seriously and in some examples the minister is even trying to push the woman in a direction contrary to that expressed in her feelings and so is more or less being openly directive in the wrong sense.

Facing Problems of Faith

The woman now has such a trusting contact with the minister that she dares to bring her real problem out into the open—I believe we can say that in this sentence the island is circumnavigated—and says: "What will God think, now that I'm so lacking in faith?"

As far as I can see this opens up two paths before the minister, both of which are valid. His choice will depend on the way he interprets this sentence. One can regard it as an expression of a definite feeling of uncertainty and even perhaps of fear which is perplexing the woman at this moment, or as a concrete question to which a definite answer is required.

A few words over each possibility. If the minister reacts to the feelings expressed, he can reflect them in a sympathetic way and say:

"You are wondering whether God will blame you for not being able to face up to this operation."

There is a considerable chance that because of the minister's acceptance of her fear, she will suddenly find her own belief rising in her and will say, "No, I believe that God will continue to regard me as a child in my weakness and forgive me." We see that in this sort of conversation where the minister dares to trust in those possibilities which are present in the patient—this trust which for Rogers is a prerequisite for any successful counseling—that deep in herself, she really does know and only needs helping in order to make her way to the light. I would also note here that what we learn for ourselves stays with us better than what is told us by someone else. We must not always suppose that we have to tell something in order to bring the other person onto the right track. If the woman has in this way found herself, the pastor, from within the light in which she now stands, can read a piece from the Bible and pray with her. Or, if the conversation has been rather tiring, just pray with her. By now he knows just what he should express in his prayer in her name.

Should the pastor take the question as a concrete one, then he must answer it adequately. Because this is a question concerning faith, the answer must also clearly be one dealing with faith. I would therefore suggest that the minister begin his answer with a phrase such as "I believe that . . ." or "We believe that. . . ." Alternatively, "In the Bible, the book of our faith, it says . . ." or "Perhaps you have sung in church. . . ." Perhaps we would differ about the closer definition of the answer, but it is clear that it should contain something about the gospel and the good message. Particularly this word "message." A message is directed to free people, to a "subject," not an "object." So in our pastoral care of this woman we will not try to push her gently in the right direction by offering categorical advice, and even less shall we make little of her feelings by using a paternal tone of voice. Thus one could certainly say: "I believe that the story of Christ in Gethsemane shows us the way here," but not: "Come, come, surely you haven't forgotten Gethsemane?"

An Exercise in Pastoral Conversation

It is not the intention of this book to give recipes. They do not exist in pastoral work, which is a creative act of two people in which not only the words but, in particular, the feelings play a great part. Such an example as this, indeed, the whole reference to Rogers and his method is only meant to help us understand answers, differentiate between mistakes, get a feeling for certain attitudes with which we are afflicted and in some blessed cases are reprieved of; in short, this book in particular aims at spurring us on to self-criticism and the sharpening of our often hesitant intuition. I must add here that I am well aware that a personal discussion with an exchange of words does get us much further than sentences on a piece of paper to which we cannot actively react. In a discussion ideas can take deeper root in us. It was while writing this book that I first fully realized how much more fruitful a week's clinical training would be than the reading of this book, in spite of the fact that there we often only get a whiff of possible problems and their solutions.

However, perhaps we can attempt to introduce into this book some self-activity which is so characteristic of clinical training, be it on a modest scale by submitting an exercise like the last one to the reader and asking him to frame a number of correct and incorrect answers. In the appendix to this chapter the reader can compare his answers with mine. In our clinical training we usually begin the day with a similar exercise. The participants write down on a piece of paper what they consider the correct and incorrect answers given by the pastor, and compare them among one another. Here then is a second conversation.

An older, unmarried woman, whose brother (whom she has cared for during the last years) died about a year ago, has asked if she may have a talk with the minister. She comes in and, when the minister has offered her a chair, she says, rather hesitantly:

"I hope you won't think me childish, Vicar, when I tell you what's on my mind."

Possible answer from the minister:
  a. empathic-reflective
  b. generalizing
  c. moralizing
  d. pushing

Woman: "It's so on my mind; I can't get over it that my brother's dead."

Possible answer from the minister:
- *a.* empathic-reflective
- *b.* generalizing
- *c.* diagnostic
- *d.* moralizing
- *e.* dogmatic
- *f.* pushing

Woman: "It seems as if life doesn't mean anything any more."

Possible answer from the minister:
- *a.* empathic-reflective
- *b.* generalizing
- *c.* interpretive
- *d.* moralizing
- *e.* dogmatizing

Woman: "When you get home, the emptiness just falls on you again."

Possible answer from the minister:
- *a.* empathic-reflective
- *b.* generalizing
- *c.* diagnostic
- *d.* moralizing
- *e.* pushing

The conversation continues for a while in this way till the woman suddenly looks directly at the minister and says:

"Is it sinful, Vicar, to sit here talking like this?"

Possible answer from the minister:
- *a.* empathic-reflective
- *b.* reacting to the content of the spoken words

c. dogmatizing
d. generalizing
e. moralizing
f. diagnosing

In the appendix (below) the reader who has answered these questions for himself can see what I had in mind when I constructed this conversation. I also hope that he will have got on far enough to be in a position to disagree with me here and there and to prefer his own replies. The value of such exercises does not lie in the fact that we learn to imitate others but that, through listening to others as painstakingly thoughtfully and critically as possible, we summon up the courage to carry out our own ideas.

One can put it this way: We can all learn from and with one another because we are learners and will always remain so. Thus I regret that I shall not see the sentences that you readers will commit to paper for I am convinced that I should learn something from them. I am more and more certain that clinical training is a process which goes on continuously.

Appendix

Here are the answers given to the questions set in the exercise in Chapter 4 as I would form them. Once more, a pastoral conversation is a personal creation, and what I give here is what I consider right or wrong in this conversation. My intention is only to provide a touchstone with which the reader can check his own answers. He must himself decide if and in what degree he agrees with my suggestions.

I shall repeat the situation as given previously. An elderly, unmarried woman, whose brother (whom she has cared for the last years) died about a year back, has asked if she may come and talk to the minister. She comes in and when the minister has offered her a seat and she has taken it, she begins to speak in a rather hesitant way.

Woman: "I hope you won't think me childish, Vicar, when I tell you what's on my mind."

Possible answer from the minister:

   a. empathic-reflective: "You are troubled by something, but you are afraid I'll think you childish."

   b. generalizing: "Lots of people are frightened that their problems will be thought childish."

   c. moralizing: "People of your age oughtn't to be scared of talking about their problems any more."

   d. pushing: "Just begin and you'll find that it all comes out of its own accord."

Woman: "It's so on my mind, I can't get over it that my brother's dead."

Possible answer from the minister:

   a. empathic-reflective: "The fact that you still can't accept your brother's death weighs on you a great deal."

   b. generalizing: "There are more people who have just these difficulties."

   c. diagnostic: "Perhaps that is an aspect of your character that you find it hard to let go of people who mean something in your life."

   d. moralizing: "After a year one really must try to have an interest in other things again."

   e. dogmatizing: "Isn't this a sign of how deeply God lays the bands of love?"

   f. pushing: "I can probably find a family where you could be a help."

Woman: "It seems to me as if life doesn't mean anything any more."

Possible answer from the minister:

   a. empathic-reflective: "So it almost seems pointless to go on living?"

   b. generalizing: "Such ideas often arise after a death."

   c. interpreting: "It seems to me that this is a symptom of being too wrapped up in yourself."

   d. moralizing: "Wouldn't it be better if you didn't think so much about the past?"

e. dogmatizing: "God is the God of the living and not of the dead."

Woman: "When you get home the emptiness just falls on you again."

Possible answer from the minister:

a. empathic-reflective: "It is so bleak at home, so lacking in human warmth."

b. generalizing: "Houses can make such an empty impression if some-one whom you loved isn't there any more."

c. diagnostic: "That's because, I fear, you are still thinking far too much about your brother."

d. moralizing: "You really must try to be a bit braver."

e. pushing: "Another parishioner got herself a dog after her husband died."

The conversation continues for some time in this way, until the woman suddenly looks straight at the minister and says: "Is it sinful, Vicar, to sit here talking like this?"

Possible answer from the minister:

a. empathic-reflective: "You are uncertain whether or not being so wrapped up in yourself is indeed sinful?"

b. reacting on the words alone: "It can be, I think, but I believe it depends on how you yourself feel about it."

c. dogmatic: "Some people differentiate between self-love and sin in this sort of case."

d. generalizing: "This sort of question often arises in the minds of people who have suffered great sorrow."

e. moralizing: "People like you who are sorrowing mustn't mention the word 'sin' too soon."

f. diagnostic: "Because you feel you have to struggle with yourself, you are afraid you'll fall into sin."

V

Appraising Pastoral
Conversation

In this chapter we want to test what we discussed in
the last chapter by looking into a number of reports of conversations held by different ministers. These reports have been collected
in various ways. Some have already been published, others have
been discussed in our clinical training sessions. The reader will
understand that it was impossible to leave the last ones unaltered.
So they have been made unrecognizable.

A Hospital Call

The first report is from a minister who knows something of
Rogers' ideas in this field and tries to apply them in practice. He
himself feels handicapped, as he remarks at the end, by the fact
that throughout the conversation he remained conscious of the
part he was trying to play. This is a hindrance which often occurs

but which most people grow out of after a while. Also, the fact that he knows the sick woman whom he visits, as the family seamstress and as someone who is no churchgoer, hinders him from being open-minded.

I shall first give the conversation in its entirety and then at the end make some remarks. I shall point out a few things which might otherwise escape attention, and which make the conversation more colorful reading. It is worth noting that, in spite of the somewhat wooden reflecting by the minister, the sick woman feels completely at ease with him and fully expresses her difficulties in the hospital. Because the minister does not criticize her but is empathic, she herself, after her initial aggression has worn off and after she has told the minister about the communion service, swings back as it were to the theme of human contacts in the hospital. It is also noticeable that at the end she signifies that she can calmly contemplate staying on in the hospital, something which you would never guess from the beginning of the conversation, and something which would have been impossible had the minister begun to discuss her objections right away. This conversation then is an example of how the minister by his empathic listening helps this woman to help herself, that is to say, to reach a deeper insight and acceptance. Here now is the report.

Mrs. W. is our sewing woman, married, and about fifty years of age. She is in the university hospital after having had more than one operation. I go to look her up. When I arrive she is walking up the corridor headed back to her room. She looks weak and sallow. Once in the ward she takes off her dressing gown and gets into bed, after first asking if I minded. As soon as she is lying down, she asks me how my wife is getting on (she, too, has just had an operation). I tell her about this, and she asks about other members of the family.

W: "I keep on vomiting; I'm still pretty poorly."
Minister: "You still feel weak?"
W: "I do get out of bed now and then but I'm still too ill for it."
M: "You feel you still can't do much."
W: "I'm all right. I don't give in."
M: "You don't worry about it at all."
W: "I have had all sorts of injections."

She now describes everything that has happened to her in some detail. A nurse comes and stands beside her and says a few encouraging words.

W: "I really like the older nurses better than these young ones. They don't care about you."
M: "They really aren't ready for caring."
W: "No, not really. They don't understand. If you've been sick, they leave the basin there under your nose. One of the older nurses would never do that. They turn the main lights slap on just as you've dropped into your first sleep. If you had thought for someone else you wouldn't do that."
M: "They aren't sufficiently thoughtful."
W: "No, but an older nurse, she sees more, takes better care of you, that's what you need."
M: "One really does like to feel that someone is thinking and caring for us."

The conversation now continues about what a certain nurse had done wrong. A little later she comes into the ward with food and is pointed out to me. Just as I am asking myself if and how I can give the conversation a more serious turn without coming outside Mrs. W.'s frame of reference and perhaps frightening her, she says: "Last Thursday we had communion here. I went, too. It was in another ward, and we were taken in our beds. Minister F.—is that his name?—led the service."

M: "So you took the opportunity of being able to make your communion?"

W: "Yes, somehow being in the hospital makes you need it more. It means more to you."

(At home, Mrs. W. is not a churchgoer.)

M: "Yes, you feel more strongly the ties of this relationship into which you are admitted."

W: "Yes, it really does you good." She is silent for a moment and then says: "That girl who's just been brought in and who's opposite here has been operated on twice. The doctors where she comes from had given her up. Now they're really managing to help her. Three months after she gets home she's going to get married. She's really looking forward to it. I go and talk to her sometimes."

M: "You take an interest in her."

W: "Yes, first she lay the other side of a screen, but I often heard her talking, because she was lying there on her own, I went over to visit her. Then I suggested to her that she should move over to our side. . . . The doctor asked my son if I'd really hoped to be home for Easter; he'd so often seen me looking out of the window he was afraid I was fretting."

M: "He probably thought you were worrying."

W: "Yes, I can quite see that. I can't go home yet. It'd cause too much trouble. My blood must be really good first. It's not too bad here."

M: "You get well taken care of here."

W: "Except the food. It's too rich for me. At home you can choose what you want, and if it's too much you can leave half for later."

M: "Now I must begin to make my way home. Would you like us to pray together?"

W: "Yes."

M: (prays) "We are safe with thee. Thou hast through Christ let us know that thou lovest us. We do not know what difficulties we still have to go through, but we believe that we always live in thy light. Be thou always with us. And with those whom we love. Give us patience and courage for the future. Amen."

W: "Give my best regards to everyone at home."

As I went away, I realized to my dismay that one of the faults of this conversation was that I had quite forgotten to ask after her family. Probably because I had been to engrossed in the part I had to play. Also, as far as pastoral work goes, more could have been made from the opening concerning the communion service.

We remarked above that the minister was handicapped by the fact that he knew his patient as the family seamstress, which made it difficult to choose between playing the role of friend or minister. It is quite understandable, therefore, that he wonders to himself— as many another minister has after visiting the sick—whether he has not fallen short as minister.

Reading the report through, we can be sure that from the moment that the sick woman begins to talk about the communion service she is regarding her visitor as a minister. It almost seems an invitation to him to take on a pastoral role toward her. The minister is clearly uncertain of what he should say, and in his reaction, "You took the opportunity of making your communion" is not sufficiently with the patient. Her information is here repeated but the feeling of thankfulness behind it is not reflected. A reply such as, "You were happy to be able to take part," would have been better. Moreover Mrs. W. does express an important feeling when she says, "Yes, somehow being in hospital makes you need it more. It means more to you." But the minister makes nothing of this when he says—too diagnostically—"Yes, you feel more strongly the ties of this relationship into which you are admitted." He is not sufficiently with her here. The result is that this theme is dropped. Had he said, "You felt that at this particular moment it held great meaning for you," doubtless an important conversation about the celebration of communion would have developed.

This visit was without doubt of considerable importance to the sick woman. She felt the interest and sympathy of the minister; she had the opportunity to have a good talk and also to let some of her inner feelings come to the light; she was able to pray in an atmosphere of devotion and, with the pastor, was able to reach a deeper insight into her being in the hospital and is now more conscious of this, though it was always present in her. But because at a certain point the minister was uncertain of himself—and was thus not sufficiently integrated—he lost an important opening in the conversation.

A Lapse into a Directive Approach

The second conversation was held by a minister who had taken part in a course of clinical training and tried seriously to put into practice what he had learned there. When he produced his report he admitted that at a certain point he no longer knew how to go on reflecting the other man's feelings and had fallen back on the well-tried directive method. He showed himself extremely interested in the comments of the group when it was analyzed. I shall report these remarks as fully as possible.

The other person in the conversation is an old man, who lives with his daughter, is a staunch churchgoer, and became ill on holiday.

Minister: "How are you getting on?"
Man: "I was taken ill on holiday, and now I've got jaundice. I hadn't been well for some days before and then one morning my children noticed how yellow I looked. The doctor in Arnhem prescribed some medicine and said I must go to my doctor at home for treatment straightaway, and here I am."
Minister: "You feel this is very hard luck."

87

This is a nice example of empathic feeling, well reflecting the sick man's feelings and giving him the impression that here is someone who takes him seriously and is prepared to listen.

Man: "Yes, I've never been ill in my life, and now this suddenly."
Minister: "You don't find it easy to accept, do you?"

Once again the feelings behind the words are well-reflected.

Man: "No. I've prayed that the Lord will make me better, and he can do it, but each morning when I wake it is all just the same. You begin to wonder then if prayer does help."

It is clear that the sick man is opening up steadily under the kindly interest of the minister, and this makes it possible for him to look deeper into his feelings. Using the obvious metaphor from Fosdick, we can say that the minister is busily sailing around the island at this moment.

Minister: "Prayerful waiting is indeed difficult."

This is a dangerous reaction. The tone of voice here is all important. Just to read this sentence one could get the impression that the minister is generalizing here and as such has lost contact with the patient. However, in the conversation with the group it turned out that the minister was still reflecting, and this was particularly clear from his tone of detached sympathy. So he is still on the right track.

Man: "Yes, we are too impatient. We've no right to be helped."

A critical point in the conversation has been reached. A definite content is stated, a conviction aired, but also a feeling stressed.

What should the minister do? He can try to stay with the patient by reflection and, by sailing round the island further, give him the opportunity to express a yet deeper feeling. Or he can accept the challenge that the other has offered and react on the words alone, running the considerable risk that the island has not been sufficiently circumnavigated and that the relationship will be lost. In the conversation with the group the minister said that at this point he no longer knew how to reflect the patient's feelings and had then done what he used to do in similar circumstances before and so had reacted on the content of the words. It is clear from the further conversation that he knew he was dealing with a representative of a fundamentalist church group with its own theological dogmas, which perhaps also tempted him to answer the way he did. It turned out in the report that this directive handling did not result in real success. This led to a heated group discussion about the problems of pastoral care for people with these or similar religious convictions. It was generally agreed that carrying out a theological discussion with them was not the way to gain success. Of course, we did not reach a solution quickly, but we all agreed that work among such groups could be more fruitful if carried out by the methods taught at clinical training.

Minister: "We have no right, but. . . ."

Anyone sensing what is going on here—and in role-playing one can experience it easily—knows that the minister has by dogmatizing, put himself apart from the patient, indeed, places himself in opposition to him. This is simply an invitation to the other man to formulate his own standpoint as clearly as possible, and the danger of a barren argument lies close at hand. The man now begins to explain his theological convictions.

Man: "Yes, God does hear prayer. I have experienced it when my wife died and I was left with the three children. . . ." [Here followed a story about the death of his wife and his own hardships as a young widower] ". . . but the Lord helped me through."

This is the one aspect of his religious convictions that coincide with the minister's.

Minister: "God did not let you down."

The man has made a statement rather than having expressed his feelings, so although it seems as if the minister is reflecting here, he is not doing much more than recalling the words of the man's statement. Anything else is hardly possible.

Man: "And he won't now either. But I do now sometimes think to myself —is salvation for me?"

Here the reverse side of his conviction is exposed. God helps in particular difficulties, but that does not mean that the man can be certain of salvation. The little word "but" indicates that the relationship made in the beginning of the talk when the minister really was with the patient is no longer present. The man is now involved in a discussion with the minister.

Minister: "It is easier to believe that God shows mercy to another than to oneself."

Here the minister shows that he is very well attuned to this sick man. He tries not to take up the challenge to pursue this discussion and thus be more openly directive, but instead feels that he must try to get near the sick man again and stand in his shoes. Perhaps he is not completely successful with his formulating for he is still generalizing too much, but it is clear that once again a better, friendlier contact is laid. Perhaps an answer such as, "Now that things seem serious, doubt creeps in," might have been better.

Man: "I pray so much, but I have no certainty."

The man clearly expresses feelings of insecurity, doubt, and a longing to rise above them. If the minister wants to help him, he must take these feelings seriously, and so must reflect.

Minister: "Where is the certainty that you used to experience—in yourself, your prayers, or in God's faithfulness? We search for it too much in ourselves and in our piety."

The minister has not reacted on the feelings presented to him but instead tries to convince the man that, religiously speaking, he is dealing with his doubt in the wrong way. Here the question must be asked why the minister leaves the right track which he had seen opening up before him in the earlier answer. It is probable that he did not feel himself sufficiently at home in this role; he still saw himself as the man who has to convince his conversational partner with words. Of course, we must admit that such an answer could be fitting if, for instance, it brings release from a situation which both parties find cramping. But the question must be asked: Has the minister indeed been so completely empathic with the other man (sailing so entirely around the island) that he can do nothing else but say the words he does? What follows does, in fact, show that he is more directive here than in that which he has empathically spoken within the man's frame of reference. This report throws a clear light on the relation of empathic listening and speaking in a pastoral conversation.

Man: "That's true, but I find it difficult."

As far as the content is concerned, the man can agree with the minister's words, but his feelings refuse to follow. The word "but" has an ominous sound that indicates that the man does not really feel understood or accepted by the minister.

Minister: "It can indeed be most awfully difficult."
Man: "Yet you can't just stop praying because you feel that you have need of the Lord."
Minister: "You couldn't manage without God."
Man: "No, without him I couldn't live."
Minister: "You couldn't do without God; might it not also be that God does not want to be without you?"

Because the minister does not go on further with the controversy but seriously tries to stand beside the patient and expresses this by showing sympathy for his feelings, their relationship is now renewed in an excellent way. The minister now tries to see how far the man can react positively to a truly pastoral message. He puts a question which underneath conceals a positive message. By so doing he comes as close as possible to the patient. However, from the man's reaction it is again revealed that, though he can agree with the minister on the intellectual level, he cannot do so in his feelings. Were the earlier attempts to convince him in a directive way influential here?

Man: "Yes, God began with me."

This formulation probably includes what has gone before but this does not mean that the man is completely sure now.

Minister: "The Lord began . . ."

Probably here where the man clearly reveals an intellectual acceptance, a reflection of the feelings—in a sentence such as "You believe that God will not desert you"—would have been better. The patient would then have felt, as it were, invited to explain his uncertainty more plainly to the minister.

Man: "And he will complete it."

Apparently the minister feels that this is too intellectually tinted; at any rate he does not follow it up.
There is silence.

Daughter: "Would you like some tea, Vicar?"
Minister: "Another time that would be very nice but not now, thank you. I've just had tea with the neighbors."
Man: "Yes, it is difficult."

For the man the difficulties are not yet solved.

Minister: "Perhaps you ought to say, that it is too difficult for *us*."

May I say that the minister is showing signs of defeat? He tries again to be directive and gets no reaction. I should like to put this question: Should one not consider such a case as this, where the patient is so strangled with his feelings of doubt, as one of counseling in Rogers' sense? In this case, the counselor carries on entirely nondirectively with his client in the belief that the client will struggle through to a liberating insight in his own deepest thoughts only if the counselor takes him completely seriously as he is. Experience is convincing that every directive push in one direction or another must give the client the feeling that he is not fully understood nor accepted in his uncertainty and despair, and in this way his resistance is strengthened. As I said, we have analyzed this case in detail in a group discussion and even in role-playing tried to relive it; our conclusion was that each active directive on the part of the minister, even in the form of *anagoge* or a theological argument, came up against resistance. Only one of the participants knew of an example where a minister who, in spite of a similar barrier, in his realization that he was dealing with a man in need, continued to visit a sick man without once showing that he was in some way or other belittling the patient's difficulties. Nevertheless, he experienced the fact that when dying the patient did surrender completely. From this we drew the conclusion that the deepened relationship brought about by these visits—if we attempt modestly to analyze psychologically what had taken place here—had created a climate where the Holy Spirit could quicken the message of the minister, which was nothing more than the message of the Bible.

Man: "Yes, that is why we must pray."
Minister: "Shall we read from the Bible what God has to say about prayer and what he promises to the man who prays?"
Man: "Yes, please, Vicar."
[The minister reads Luke 18:1-8; he repeats the last words "will not God vindicate his elect? . . . I tell you, he will vindicate them speedily."]
Man: "Yes, the Lord is good."
Minister: "Would you like us to thank him together and lay down this conversation we've had before him?"
Man: "Yes, please."
[We then prayed together.]
Man: "Yes, surely the Lord will work for the best . . . but sometimes it is difficult."

When the man says that we must pray because this is difficult for us, the minister seizes the opportunity to read aloud from the

Bible. He repeats the last words with emphasis. I do not think that it is wrong to say that the minister, now that his attempts to break through the sick man's resistance have failed, tries to influence him directively via the Bible. But in this way the message of the Bible does not become liberating, and the man once more confirms in an intellectual way what the minister tries to make clear to him, yet ends with the words "But sometimes it is difficult." Thus a real liberation has not been achieved.

The most important things which can be said about this conversation have been mentioned above. Here I only want to add a few remarks. In this conversation the minister shows himself to be a man who earnestly does his best to help the sick man. He does not become irritated, nor does he take an authoritarian attitude; one continually gets the impression that he wants to stand beside this sheep of his flock in a loving and careful way. If we now put the question, "Why did not this conversation lead to a truly satisfactory result?" then we must point out two factors which depend on each other closely. In the first place, the minister by reflecting, begins to work his way into the feelings of this sick man and so to encourage him into embarking onto a really worthwhile conversation. But, in one way or another, he does not know how to sustain his part of being the helpful listener and switches over to being a helpful theologian—really before the sick man has laid bare the deepest doubts of his heart. Secondly, because of this the conversation now becomes a sort of discussion in which the minister says some very good things, which, however, fail to hit their mark. Of course, we can only guess how this conversation might have developed had the minister continued to play his first role carefully and lovingly. Perhaps he would not have made his mark in one visit, perhaps psychotherapeutic help from an expert was necessary. But I will risk making the suggestion that this conversation shows us the limitations of the directive approach in the technical, Rogerian (thus not prophetic) sense of the word, with the additional indication that a nondirective phase in a conversation opens the way to a contact in which more profound pastoral possibilities become visible.

A Home Call by an Untrained Pastor

I shall now give a report of a conversation of a minister who had had absolutely no training in the fundamentals of carrying out a pastoral conversation. I should like to make a few introductory remarks. In this book we have seen that it is of great importance in the carrying out of conversations that a minister should have the right attitude. We have determined that this attitude can be described as "being with the other man," an attitude that realizes itself in listening empathically and which is supported and deepened by the reflection of the other man's feelings. I should like to draw attention to the fact that this reflection, which for Rogers is the most important tool in his psychotherapy, is an aid used in pastoral conversations to make that contact which opens the way for a true pastoral message.

In this conversation there is no question of reflection. There appears to be a good relationship between the minister and his parishioner, but one gets the feeling that the contact made between them in this conversation is never deepened into a real pastoral contact. Too little empathy seems to exist, and because of this there seems to be a certain tendency to well-meant directive behavior which does not really hit home. My impression is that the attitude is pastoral in intention but is not worked out either technically or profoundly enough. I shall limit my remarks about this conversation to a few notes which in particular throw light on the minister's attitude.

Mrs. F. (aged about fifty) has been bedridden with osteoarthritis for some years. Some time before she had still been able to get out and about in a wheelchair or in her self-drive invalid car. The family consists of her husband and two sons in their early twenties. As I had not been to see her for a long time, I did not exactly know how she was.

Woman: "How nice that you have come again!"

Minister: "Are you quite confined to bed nowadays, or do you still sometimes use your wheelchair?"

Woman: "Hardly ever now. If I do, it takes so much effort it really isn't worth it."

Minister: "Is it very hard being confined to your bed?"

Woman: "I do think it's awful that I can't get to church anymore, and it's a pity I can't get out in my car anymore—but I've accepted it completely."

It is strange that the minister asks so many questions. Putting too many questions in a pastoral conversation is dangerous; one so speedily finds oneself standing opposite rather than beside the other person, and so, as it were, dictating the direction the conversation takes instead of giving the other person the opportunity to take a look at his inner life, when by so doing we might be able to help him. However, from the friendly way the minister refers to this woman in his report, it seems apparent she is aware of his interest in her. It is because of this flourishing relationship that she does not only answer the content of the questions but also reveals some of her deeper feelings.

Mrs. F. grew up in a loving, pious atmosphere and kept this temperament through those years when she was still healthy. She speaks about this time with special thankfulness. She remembers a verse her grandmother had written; she lovingly recalls an uncle and aunt who died recently, after being taken ill on holiday. She has always had a trait of pure childishness, and due to her sickness this has increased somewhat.

Minister: "Your life must be much lonelier."
Woman: "Yes, the journey to the grave is short."
[with shining eyes, she says:]

> The path your Savior trod
> Of daily toil and woe,
> Wait but a little while
> In uncomplaining love,
> His own most gracious smile
> Shall welcome you above.

Minister: "It must certainly be a pleasure for you to know so many verses by heart."
Woman: "Yes. I get an enormous amount out of it. I learned so many hymns in my childhood. It's so useful now that I get so tired from reading."

I am impressed by the way the minister keeps up his attitude of friendly interest. He keeps a certain distance and does not come nearer. I wonder whether he could not have deepened this relationship had he reflected the woman's feelings and so by entering them begun to feel with her. The questions now take a turn in the direction of mild diagnostic interest, but the minister does not get any nearer the woman herself. In a certain sense this conversation could equally well have taken place between the woman and a trusted family doctor. I think that it is difficult to develop a real pastoral conversation from this sort of relationship.

Minister: "Am I right in thinking that you set more store in hymns than in the psalms? But don't you think that the ups and downs of life come out better in the psalms than in the hymns which are more equable?"
Woman: "There *are* splendid psalms [She quotes some verses from Psalm 73], but you know how attached I am to the hymns!"

Minister: "But just think of Psalm 73; there in the beginning you find all sorts of riddles about life. [The woman quotes the text he means.] The poet has had some difficulty in solving them all."
Woman: "I, too, find life a puzzle—just to think of my lying here in this small corner! But still—believe me—I have learned to see beyond it."

We must admire the subtle, cautious manner that the minister uses to discover how far or whether there is a possibility or need in the woman for a more pastoral conversation. But, in Rogers' terms, he deals directively here—even pushingly—however wary he is. And strangely enough the result is the same as in the previous conversation; the woman follows the minister into the intellectual sphere and admits that for her, too, life is a riddle. But by her clear "But still . . ." she reveals that she has accepted his point rationally but not with her feelings. The minister did not speak as a result of empathically listening (the island was not sufficiently circumnavigated), therefore he was not within her frame of reference (was not "with" her), and the result is that here too a discussion threatens to develop. The minister, who throughout this conversation shows himself to be friendly and not at all an authoritarian person, seems to grasp that he must not take the path he sees opening before him.

Minister: "It will surely interest you to hear that the new versification of the psalms is out now. They should now mean much more to people."
Woman: "Possibly, but they won't say much to me. I have such a reservoir into which I can dip, that it's really enough for me."
Minister: "But then you will again and again discover how much it means to you to be alive still."

Am I right when I seem to notice that the minister draws nearer to the woman at this point? Obviously he is now within her frame of reference and tries—without the silent criticism which seemed implicit in the preceding part—to really help her. This is not pushing, but liberating; not authoritarian, but said in the attitude of being with the other person. The woman reacts very positively.

Woman: "Sometimes I have the feeling that Paul had—'to be free from this world with Christ is best'—but the purpose of my life lies in the fact that again and again I can be of use in comforting people." [Here she mentions several names of people with whom she often talks.]
Her husband comes in. He is a more down-to-earth character, though their relationship is a good one.
Husband: "Don't get too overly spiritual, mind!"
Minister: "We've just been talking about how your wife can be such a help to others in her present position."
They talk further about the children.
Minister: "I'm glad I could come and talk to you again."
Woman: "I hope you'll come again."

A question now forces its way up—might not some training considerably have helped a minister such as this? Am I far wrong when I suggest that this is almost a copybook example of the way in which many ministers carry out pastoral conversations? This pastor is prepared for contact with and helpfulness toward the other person, but because he is not conscious of his role and thus not of his attitude and supporting techniques, openings in the conversation are neglected and by well-meant but directive behavior obstacles for a fruitful development of the conversation are created.

A Good Conversation

This report is also from a minister who had never heard of clinical training, reflection, etc. I give it here because, in spite of the fact that he has fairly obviously sinned against certain rules of technique, it is in many ways a good conversation. The sick woman who took part in it also says it had helped her. In this book we have more than once shown that the making of the relationship is more important than the technique for success, and I think that this conversation is a convincing proof of this statement. Two things must be said in order to understand this conversation properly. Firstly, this minister has a particularly calm, warmhearted, "safe" personality and is therefore more cut out for building up a good relationship than many another; secondly, although one can point to some technical deficiencies, he is never directive in the wrong sense of the word. He possesses the attitude of being with the other person quite apart from any technique.

Miss B. is a young woman, twenty-three years old, unmarried, a house-mother at a children's home. I visited her as a patient in the hospital where I was chaplain. I had not come across her before. She lay in bed, made a cheerful impression, and was talkative. She answered my question if I might introduce myself by saying:

Miss B: "I recognize you from the church service. I was there last Sunday."
Pastor: "Oh, were you there? That's nice. Then I'm already a bit of an acquaintance to you."
Miss B: "Yes. And I have already had a visit from Minister X. Do you know him? I was prepared for confirmation by him."
Pastor: "I know several ministers of that name but probably a generation older than the one you mean. I knew one in Assen, one in Amsterdam, and one in Zwolle."
Miss B: "No, my Minister X. certainly won't be one of them. He's a youth minister. I have had some trouble with my fiancé, but luckily that's over. Now I only have to get calm again. That's why I'm here. I do so wish I could have my own room, but the doctors prefer it like this. I'm absolutely sure it would be better for me if I were alone."
Pastor: "Have you been engaged long?"

Following the rules of the technique, the minister here would do best to reflect the feelings which the patient reveals. By asking this question he breaks the flow of feelings. Probably the patient feels in the tone of voice in which this question was put that the minister is not belittling her difficulties, but rather by this question is actually trying to draw nearer the better to understand her problems. Perhaps he feels more or less intuitively that she was too effusive in the expression of her feelings and that without hurting her he would do best to keep the conversation in an objective, calm atmosphere. The feelings will begin to flow again, and perhaps then they will do so in a more adequate way. Problems like these may arise in a pastoral conversation.

Miss B: "Not so long. About a year. We'd known each other a bit longer, but after my father died we became officially engaged."
Pastor: "Did the difficulties begin soon after that?"

The minister has made a definite diagnosis to himself and wants to verify it. To my way of thinking this taking up a diagnostic position in a pastoral conversation is not right, but here again it is not regarded as an obstacle in the way of the relationship but rather as an addition to that relationship. The sick woman takes this question as a sign of real, not mere diagnostic, interest, and the conversation continues without any further difficulty.

Miss B: "Yes, it happened more or less simultaneously. My mother was left with three children; one was already married and a younger brother was at home."
Pastor: "You went to confirmation classes with Minister X.?"

It is worth noticing that the minister does not go on with his diagnosis. He feels that he is not on the right track. This question

102

does not seem very relevant yet fits in in the way in which he shows his interest, and so, far from harming the relationship, adds to its construction.

Miss B: "Yes, he could do that, even though he was youth minister."
Pastor: "Do you go to communion if it is celebrated?"

One would like to know why the minister puts this question. It could be from real pastoral interest, and the tone in which it was spoken would show this and so advance the relationship. It could have been to give the conversation a certain pastoral shape and can on this point be defended, though it would have been more sensible to have let the patient know from the beginning of the visit what he had really come for as chaplain. It could also be an introduction to an invitation to take part in the next celebration of communion, but this would then have come better at the end of the conversation. I have a feeling that the minister put this question almost out of a sense of duty, because he had no clear idea of what his role as pastor involved. Because he has such a "safe" personality and the question betrays so real an interest, the patient probably does not feel it to be either inquisitorial or threatening. At least she goes on talking with no difficulty. However, the conversation is in danger of being sidetracked. Apparently the patient does not clearly see what the minister is driving at.

Miss B: "I always hesitate a bit, but I haven't given it up. And I always tell the children about the dear Lord, and they do so like to listen. Just imagine what one of them said when I left to come here—she said, 'Don't stay away long because you must read aloud more of the exciting adventures of our dear Lord!' Don't you thing that's a striking remark from a tiny mite from a children's home?"
Pastor: "Yes, more like an adult's remark."

Miss B: "I love the way the children from the home are so interested."
[Here a conversation develops about retelling stories from children's
Bibles to young children and about their reactions to them.]
Pastor: "Of course you've discussed your problems with the doctors and
Minister X. You wouldn't feel the need to talk to me about them. Have
you had a special training for your work?"

I wonder why the minister asked this. Does he have the feeling
that he has not yet hit on a point in his questioning from which a
pastoral conversation could be developed? One would imagine so
after his remark about discussing her difficulties. It is clear enough
that he is a retiring man and does not want to force himself
on this young woman who has already been visited by the minister
who prepared her for confirmation. But perhaps it is just this
unpretentiousness which gives the patient the feeling that here
is someone with whom she can talk. The minister's questions indicate continually that he wants to keep his distance from her, but
the tone of his words, the modest seriousness of his behavior, the
feeling of security which streams from him gives her the courage
to get things off her chest. One notices how the feelings start to flow
again, as it were, unstimulated.

Miss B: "Yes, I did a course at the school of social studies. I got to know
my fiancé during the first months. He fell in love with me straightaway,
but I didn't dare take up with him. He was don't-carish and rough on the
outside. I hoped that it was just superficial but wanted to be certain of
this. He was completely indifferent and hard as far as religion was concerned. That's now completely changed; it's really a marvel! I suggested
a probation time of six months for us both to make completely sure of
ourselves. During this time, however, he was in contact with another girl
—against our agreement. He took her out several times, though they
never became very intimate. I found out about this and wrote to say I
didn't want him anymore, though I must say it was only then that I

realized I loved him more than I'd thought. It was an awful blow to him. But luckily it's all gone well again now. I was terribly insensitive then. Now it's much better than we ever thought it could be. Later on he told me—maybe you think this is a bit absurd—that he had felt awfully lonely and that I was really that girl; he'd love her because he saw me in her."

Pastor: "I think I understand all right."

Miss B: "And now I'm here although I feel very well and everything is going well between us. The doctor wants to know why I reacted in such a very extreme way about these difficulties in my engagement. But a conversation with Minister X. or with you—if I get to know you better—helps more than one with the psychiatrists."

Pastor: "I can quite understand that you'd like a room to yourself and hope you'll get one shortly. But now I must make room for the doctor for the nurse has signed that he's on his way."

There is no reflecting in this conversation. Yet, it was a particularly liberating one as we can see from the girl's own words. If she says so, it is not for us to think otherwise. In this chance encounter between hospital chaplain and young patient, who has already had a pastoral visit, the minister has given what he felt he ought to give: a sincere interest and concern for the patient's difficulties. This loving care came from a consistently good attitude of being "beside" the other person without being directive in the wrong way. Had the minister been more empathic and known the technique of reflecting, and so asked fewer questions, perhaps the conversation would have shown greater depth and less fortuity, but the pastor's interest was apparently so lively that the girl could do precisely what she needed, namely, have her say.

A Venture Beyond the Nondirective

The following report is from a minister who had participated in a course of clinical training and who consequently tried to be nondirective. So he begins by reflecting and afterwards tries to move over to a pastoral conversation in the real sense of the phrase.

In an Amsterdam hospital he comes accidentally into contact with an apparently extremely lonely man who, under the sincere interest of the minister, thaws out and unburdens himself. The "pastoral" part fits well into the conversation as a whole and the minister is definitely not directive, but one gets the impression that the chance to talk to a minister means a very great deal to this man and that the explicit talk about faith is more a clarification than a liberation. The transition from pastoral in the general sense to pastoral in its narrower meaning—that is to say, from reflecting to preaching the gospel message—has different aspects which could only be brought clearly into relief after more empirical study and working out of principles than we are able to do here.

The report is as follows:

Mr. P. is a man of sixty who has been taken into hospital for observation. He suffers from stomach trouble and for some years now has been coming into hospital for checks. At first sight, he seems to feel at home, a well-dressed, tall man sitting in a chair. He is astonished when I tell him my name; he thinks that a minister will be coming to visit him from Hilversum, his hometown.

Mr. P: "I don't know a minister of your name in Hilversum."
Pastor: "No, I live in Amsterdam and visit hospital patients here. What's your trouble?"
Mr. P: "Stomach, I've been here two weeks under observation."
Pastor: "You came from Hilversum?"
Mr. P: "Yes, I've lived there the last twenty years. My wife died twelve years ago. She was nursed in the T. B. sanatorium for the last months. Yes, I've known some troubles."

It is noticeable how the man reveals important information about himself without the minister asking questions. Just because he does not ask them but more or less unconsciously stands next to the patient, the man feels it is pleasant to tell the minister something about himself.

Pastor: "You have had a lot of dark patches in your life."
Mr. P: "Yes. I was forty-three when my daughter was born. My wife was divorced, a Roman Catholic actually. Now you know what that means. People were terribly critical. I never understood it."
Pastor: "You felt very isolated."

Anyone sympathetic to the dynamic of this conversation will see that each reflection of this man's feelings is an invitation to him to go on further. He senses that the minister is following his thoughts and goes on telling his story.

Mr. P: "Yes, the ministers know all about that. Particularly Minister B. who lives in Hilversum now. He came specially from Utrecht to visit me." [This led to a short conversation about Minister B. and others.]
Pastor: "Have you been in contact with the church here?"

In the light of the development of the conversation, this question is not directive; it is more a question by which the situation is going to be clarified. It is, as it were, an invitation to the man to say how he is getting on here in the hospital; an attempt to get closer to him. He senses this and so reveals more valuable material in the following sentences.

Mr. P: "I wanted to go to the service here in the hospital on Sunday, but there was something organized here in this part of the building for the men who were going home."
Pastor: "Yes."

The minister shows his appreciation of the situation and encourages him to go on. Such a "yes" is occasionally most effective in pastoral conversations.

Mr. P: "I didn't really dare. I'm much too sensitive. My daughter's the same. I think I've kept it from my youth."
Pastor: "You feel that ever since your youth it has marked your life."
Mr. P: "Yes. I was the youngest. Perhaps that was it. Then everything is decided for you. I think my daughter inherited it from me."
Pastor: "You've an idea that your daughter got it from the family, too."
Mr. P: "Yes, the headmistress of the high school said she'd never have an easy life."
[He explains what has happened to her and that things are better now.]
Pastor: "I can imagine that your belief helps you greatly in your troubles."

The minister here makes the effort to bring the conversation over to more pastoral ground. He throws out this suggestion to deepen the conversation, but in such a way that the man is free to follow it up or not as he wants. He asks no question and is thus not inquisitorial, nor does he say it in such a way as to make it sound directive. The suggestion arises, as it were, organically from the development of the conversation. The minister is "with" the man and stays there. The suggestion makes the impression of being diagnostic, but it is not born from objective observation. On the contrary, it is an attempt along the lines shown above to bring the man to a more profound understanding of himself, in which the minister does not suggest that he understands more of him than the man himself. However, there is a danger that he is now outside the man's frame of reference. The answer shows us that this danger is not purely imaginary.

Mr. P: "Yes, in spite of my sins."
Pastor: "You feel your sins heavily."

The minister tries to follow him empathically in his change of feelings, and so drops the theme he had begun. He might have tried to push him in the direction which he had indicated—a talk about the support faith gives in the face of life's troubles. But then he would have been directive and without a doubt this would have awakened feelings of rejection in the man. By his suggestion the minister has, so to speak, pointed out a dry riverbed into which the flow of his feelings can make its way, and it seems advisable now to follow this flow rather than dam it off.

Mr. P: "Yes, I was married to a divorced woman. But looking back on my life, I also had many blessings, many fantastically fine things happened—my daughter, and the fact that things are going so well for her now."

Pastor: "So you also see plenty of light."

Mr. P: "Yes, particularly in my daughter. I would like to go on living for her sake."

Pastor: "She gives you a purpose in life."

Mr. P: "Yes. I wouldn't mind dying much. But she needs a home. That's how I've always seen it. She always had a hard time. My wife was poorly for years before it actually came to a head and she had to go into the sanatorium."

Pastor: "It was only then that you knew she had T.B."

Here the minister has not had a chance to remain really empathic in the swift change of feelings expressed, and though it seems as if he is reflecting here, in fact he is not.

Mr. P: "People sometimes have to go through a lot alone."

The man reacts with a generalization. The minister, who feels that the relationship is broken and that the talk had better come

109

to a close, tries again to bring up the theme of the support of faith and thus to bring the conversation to a pastoral end.

Pastor: "But I imagine that it helped you to know that God, the great Other, was there. Even when you were alone among everyone else."
Mr. P: "Yes, I have often felt that."

This end is obviously too directive. The man does not contradict but feels no need to react more positively to these words. He accepts the interest taken in him, but this ending has not brought any inward liberation, any real spiritual guidance.

Pastor: "Would you like us to pray together?"
Mr. P: "Yes, I would."
Pastor: [Prays] "We often go through dark difficulties. But our strength and comfort is that we may believe that everything is contained within the peace of your hand. Every path along which we walk leads to your light, and brings us at the last to you. We thank you for being there and that, believing, we may still speak with you. Amen."
"Now I'll say good-bye. I hope you'll soon be better and quickly home."
Mr. P: "Thank you very much. I liked having this visit very much."
Pastor: "Good, and so you see the church has also been with you here in hospital."

I want to make one more remark about the end of this conversation. We saw at the beginning, in the introduction to the report, that the minister tried in the second half of the talk to give it a pastoral flavor in the narrower sense of the word, and in a non-directive way, but that one got the impression that talking outright about faith meant less to the man than the chance to be able to talk about himself to a minister. The minister was sensible enough not to press his point and, at the end when the man expresses his thanks, nicely sums up the result in the words "The church has also been with you in hospital," and so in these circumstances, too, has stood with him. I can imagine that the minister, when looking back over this conversation might feel some doubt in his own mind as to whether he made enough of the pastoral side of the conversation. I personally think that the course of the talk in which, in general, there is such a good relationship, shows that this was just what the man needed at that moment, and that had the minister tried to make "more" of the conversation, he would have been wrongly directive and would doubtlessly have spoiled the relationship and so, too, the talk.

I would repeat in this connection what I wrote above: the switch over from pastoral in the general sense to pastoral in its specialized sense, from reflecting to preaching the gospel, has several aspects which can only be brought into relief by more empirical study and deeper thinking about principles. We are certainly not yet so far that we can make a clear pronouncement about this changeover. I would just like to say that it must leave a great deal to intuition grounded on the right attitude toward both the patient and ourselves.

A Trained Roman Catholic Chaplain

Our last report is from one of the Roman Catholic members of a course we held and was made during this course. He has seriously tried to bring into practice what he has learned, and is particularly successful in this. One sees how a warm relationship and a good conversation are constructed by a simple but friendly reflection of feelings, from which the pastoral aspect in its specialized sense grows up unforced. The report is as follows:

111

A girl of about twenty-two or three has been in a neurosurgical ward for at least six weeks. I visit her at least twice a week. A friendly, personal relationship has grown up between us. She was first operated on on her arm; the nerves settled well. Two weeks later she was operated on on her neck. Since then she has lain with her head held fast in an apparatus on which weights are hung. She comes from a good family, well-educated, and also deeply religious. She still lives at home, helping her mother. Her sister, who is somewhat younger than her and to whom she is devoted, is lying dangerously ill in another hospital. The patient is engaged to be married. I come up to her in the ward and give her my hand.

She: "You *are* late."

I: "I've been on a course with some colleagues."

[We chat about this for a while.]

She: "I've been looking out for you all day."

I: "How are things going?"

This question, which brings both of them closer to each other, fits very well into their relationship.

She: "All right."

I: "Things are going fairly well."

She: "Well, I've got an awful lot of pain in my head again."

I: "More pain than last time."

[That was on Easter eve.]

She: "Yes. And now there's something else, too. I have a festering place on my head, and I don't know whether to tell my father or not. He'll be coming for a visit in a minute or two."

I: "So you don't know what to do."

Excellently reflected; the temptation to be directive has been withstood.

She: "I'd rather not tell him."

I: "Then don't yet—they have so much to bear just now."

112

In the girl's words the accent falls on a factual remark and less on her feelings; reflection here would have been artificial. This is very well sensed by the chaplain. He does little more than agree with the girl's remark and so supports her in her uncertainty. One could call this being directive, but in the relationship of dependence of this sick girl to her surroundings it fits the situation well. Moreover, the confessional creates a relationship between confessant and father confessor which Protestantism hardly knows, and such mild "directive" instructions work normally without raising any problems. One senses in his words and by the tone of his voice that he is completely "with" the girl.

She: "That's just what I was thinking. I'll wait; I can bear it."

This answer shows that the chaplain's statement has not been received as directive in the wrong sense.

I: "So you can still stick it out."

Well reflected.

She: "Yes, for last week I was much strengthened."
I: "You were given strength through the suffering of Christ."

Here it is striking indeed how the girl herself brings the conversation round to a pastoral sphere which is successfully picked up by the pastor.

She: "Yes, I found a great deal of support in it."
I: "So you've been thinking a lot about it and perhaps feel that you are suffering with him."

This is no diagnosis or interpretation but a clarification of the feelings expressed—thus, reflection.

She: "Yes, and I still have that feeling and can comfort myself with it."

The girl has clearly experienced the priest's remark as reflection and so shows a new aspect of her inner feelings.

I: "Would you like to receive the Great Comforter tomorrow? (Holy Communion.)
She: "Very much, please."
Then we say good-bye, shake hands, and I make the sign of the Cross on her forehead.

In my opinion, this conversation gives a particularly good example of what we mean by the pastoral attitude. The transition from reflecting to being pastoral in the narrower meaning of the word takes place without difficulty; the island has been completely circumnavigated and the landing made at the right place—if we can use this matter-of-fact metaphor for such a moving conversation. I believe that in this report we can see the great advantages of a course of clinical training in a hospital. Those who by an analysis of such a conversation gain insight into what the pastoral attitude implies gain in sensitivity.

VI

Psychological Aims and Modes
of Pastoral Conversation

In all pastoral conversation the primary aim of the pastor is to help the other person see his life in God's light. In this short sentence we may summarize the essence of the pastoral conversation. In its shortness it sounds very "simple" (in a way, in the deep, true meaning of the word, it is), but at the same time it is so comprehensive that life with all its heights and depths, its complications and problems, is involved. In order to get to the heart of this—to see oneself in God's light, to know life as a gift and a charge of God—a long way has to be covered in the pastoral conversation. The person we meet has not only lost his contact with God, but also with himself and his fellow man. He has become a problem for himself and in his relation with his fellow man. All this may be deeply connected with, and be an expression of, the difficulty that he no longer sees himself in God's light.

In pastoral conversation we want to help him find again a good relationship with himself, with his fellow man, with God. But along the way, as this book has stressed more than once, a more "therapeutic phase" in the pastoral conversation can be of great importance for this purpose. By this I mean that the pastor must not take a stab at what he says to people about their often so complicated life problems, and neither should he only play it by common sense or intuition; but he should also be fully alive to the importance of what he does in his conversation. To this difficult work the pastor must bring a systematic, well-considered point of view. Just as he does it for sermons and his confirmation classes, so he should do it for his conversations. When the pastor discusses someone's problems in this way, I would call this a therapeutic phase in the conversation, in which much may happen that is of great importance to the person. In this way he experiences new possibilities of human contact. He learns to face his difficulties in a different manner. An inner development is started. He discovers aspects of himself which previously he was not clearly conscious of. Also, at this therapeutic stage he may experience God's love and patience in this relationship with the pastor.

In this therapeutic stage of the pastoral conversation there are certain psychological modes and aims which are apt to be of particular value. We will limit ourselves to those which may be of direct importance for the ordinary parish pastor, so that we will pass over the specifically therapeutic modes where this does not apply—for instance, psychoanalysis, hypnosis, etc. Rümke's discussion of therapeutic modes and aims in general medical practice [1] has been of significant help in our discussion of this subject as it applies especially to the pastorate.

Abreaction—"Getting It Off the Chest"

In the first place, there is the possibility that pastoral conversation may give someone who has serious problems the chance to get

[1] H. C. Rümke, *Psychiatrie I* (Amsterdam, 1954), pp. 341-59.

it off his chest. Sometimes this may be enough. The motive for such an "abreaction" may be the more sudden acute problems—for instance, the loss of a dear one, a "moral hangover," disappointment after a broken engagement—as well as tensions and conflicts which have been there for a much longer time. The pastoral conversation then relaxes and gives the courage to continue. This may seem a very simple method of conversation to the pastor, but that is not the case. The condition is that the pastor listens quietly, in a relaxed and unprejudiced manner, and gives the other person the feeling of being unconditionally accepted regardless of what he says. I remember an unmarried woman who after much hesitation decided to speak with her physician about her masturbation problems. When she brought this matter up, she noticed for one short moment something of surprise on his face ("Does she have problems like these? I had not expected this.") He regained control of his face immediately, but it was enough to block the further conversation.

During such an abreaction the other person may become very emotional. Then it is important that the pastor maintain enough distance and not permit himself to be carried away by the emotions of the other person. Often it is well that the pastor says little in such a situation, even though he may give some quiet guidance by putting in a word if necessary. It also may be necessary to quiet and calm a person who gets too excited during the abreaction. It usually is not necessary, often undesirable, to ask for a lot of details. Our wanting to have a complete picture of the events may not be of any influence.

Such an abreaction may be a matter of one or more conversations. And it frequently involves much more than a mere abreacting of tensions or discharging of emotions. I remember a conversation with a director of a large concern, a typical manager, who suffered

117

e chilliness of his marriage, but who never could ex-
d for warmth and love. In a more or less accidental
ı, in which his marriage happened to be mentioned, he
sudden, broke out in tears. His deep-felt needs and cravings,
which he never could express and which he always had suppressed,
became too much for him. In the following part of the conversation
he arrived at a more fertile clarification of the situation which
enabled him to find a more realistic attitude. Such a possibility
for abreaction, even if it is only one conversation, can be very important. A person may have been living in an ever increasing isolation with his difficulties for a long time, and now rediscovers the
possibility of discussing all this in contact with another person, so
that the whole situation looks different.

It is of great importance that at the end of the abreaction, as
described, pastor and parishioner together try to see the problems
in God's light, to stand together in God's presence, probably also
through prayer. If we leave it as just an opportunity for abreaction,
then it may be of great value, but as a pastor we fall short of our
task. We have let the person down, because we did not sufficiently
assimilate and accept his problems in faith. Of course, we should
be warned that we must not be led into a rigid pastoral procedure
but must always maintain a free creative attitude toward the other
in this pastoral encounter.

Suggestion and the Suggestive Element in the Pastoral Conversation

Here we have a mode of conversation which has been important
in pastoral care in different ways. First of all, it has played a role
in psychotherapy and has been used there in the sense of a con-

sciously pursued, independent method, systematically and consistently applied.

The form of suggestion which may be considered as a specific psychotherapeutic method was especially propagated by the theory and practice of men such as A. A. Liébeault (1823-1904) and E. Coué (1857-1926). It implies a systematic and purposive authoritarian attitude and intends to effect, by continuously repeated words, a change in the ways of thinking and feeling, possibly to start a psychic process. No effort is made to appeal to the personal, critical, or emotional cooperation of the other person. The therapist uses the need and tendency of the person toward dependence on others, his docility and submissiveness, but does not pursue the free personal cooperation of the client. They do not arrive at a real dialogue. Rather it is a monologue with a compelling and submitting character.

It is evident that besides this systematic application as an independent form of psychotherapy, suggestion may also play a more or less important part in other forms of therapy; in particular, in the psychoanalytic situation and method this may be the case more so than perhaps many realize. The explanation and interpretation of all sorts of material according to rigid schemes may assume the character of almost systematic suggestion.

The success of suggestion can at first appear considerable, but, indeed, it only appears that way. More than once the significance of suggestive reassurance has been pointed out in attaining a lessening of anxiety and guilt feelings, in gaining more distance from emotions, in finding the rest desirable for recovery, etc. There may be some truth in it and, because of that, a certain justification of a suggestive attitude in some situations. But in any case no permanent result is reached in deeper feelings of anxiety and guilt, no permanent relief, improvement or peace of mind. Perhaps we all know examples of people who come into the sphere of some spiritual revival movement and come into contact with a pastor who has a strongly suggestive pastoral attitude. They then go home very enthusiastic because they had been relieved from anxieties, tensions, guilt feelings; but, after some time, completely slide back.

In the meantime it has become evident from the above that—beside suggestion in the narrower sense of purposely and systematically applied suggestion, which we have to reject in both psychotherapy and pastoral care—we may also speak of suggestion in a much broader sense and may ask to what extent a suggestive element may be justified and useful in pastoral conversation. This suggestion in a broader sense is based on the influence of the pastor on the conscious and, in particular, unconscious feelings of dependency of the other person.

Now I think that this suggestive element in the first place is involved (whether we like it or not) by virtue of the office of the pastor and everything that is associated with it. Official robes, of course, strengthen this suggestive element. The pastor is by virtue of his office a person toward whom people often develop feelings of dependency. He preaches the Word, he administers the sacraments (and often is especially authorized to do so), he time and time again is involved at decisive moments, often says a very meaningful word at birth and baptism, at marriage ceremonies, at times of illness, death and funerals, or in various critical situations. This suggestive element, which is inherent to his office, is influenced by the consequences of the crisis surrounding the ministry. Uncertainty and devaluation in regard to the work of the pastor diminishes the suggestive "power" for many. In so far as the suggestion still functions, it has more to do with this particular person and because of that is a factor which is difficult to "grasp." This pastor has authority for a certain person, not only because he is a pastor, but because he is at the same time a pastor and, for instance, this fine fellow whom you can trust! And the suggestive meaning of it is connected with both factors, especially in their combination.

What can we say about the suggestive element, in this broader sense, within the pastorate? Doubtless many pastors frequently use it; they try with a certain authority to reassure, to encourage, to give advice. In my opinion it is often a dubious procedure, both from a pastoral and a psychological point of view. This may be already evident from the foregoing. But then there is the *legitimate* "speaking with authority" in which we cannot deny (psychologically speaking) the presence of a suggestive element. The only one who really did it with absolute right was he about whom the gospel says, that he spoke and taught as one having authority and not as the scribes. How often did he not speak such words as: "Be of good courage." "Fear not." "Go, and sin no more"? So, we see the New Testament contains many strongly suggestive words, words based on the unconscious feelings of the believer. Indeed, the Christian knows himself to be dependent on the Lord and his strength. At the same time we feel how careful the pastor (whose speaking can only become a "speaking with authority" in commission of Christ, and therefore in a secondary manner) must be, not to be suggestive in a wrong way. But, keeping this in mind, if we want to allot a place to the suggestive element in the pastoral conversation, the following remarks may serve as a guide.

1. We should not use our pastoral influence in a suggestive way in order to avoid a more difficult but necessary pastoral conversation. And in this connection I also remark: The suggestive attitude has to be authentic, an expression of what we really *mean* to be and say. Not just something to try out for once, no gimmick, not a technical trick ("Let's see whether it works").

2. Suggestive pastoral influence must also be used in such a

way that we do not interfere between God and the other person illegitimately. The danger threatens here that the person may become dependent on the pastor in the wrong way, or that the pastor himself may make the person dependent on him. We make ourselves indispensable by a suggestive influence and stand in God's way. To give an example: If someone suffers under the knowledge of having sinned, we may prevent him from accepting his guilt in faith by a suggestive-encouraging method of speaking—for instance, by treating the significance of his deeds as of little importance—in our desire to help him. It is a poor help. But it is also possible to overemphasize the guilt of certain very unimportant matters by a suggestive pastoral attitude so that they become sources of anxiety and remorse.

3. We have to be attentive to which measure and in which way we use the suggestive element in the conversation. There are certain, often very simple, parishioners who expect the suggestive, authoritative attitude in a pastoral conversation and to whom it would be an injustice if we did not respond in a spiritually justified manner. But with others it would have an adverse effect again. I recall a simple elderly woman whose adult son, himself also a Christian, had been cremated, and who worried a lot about it because Roman Catholic and Protestant acquaintances had told her that this was a grave sin, possibly unpardonable—because no repentence was possible any more! In this case one single pastoral conversation in which the suggestive element was not lacking was sufficient to put her mind at ease. It stands to reason that if a suggestive element in the pastoral conversation is used, this suggestive pastoral manner of speaking has to refer to something that is true and that is also possible. This presupposes that the pastor knows the situation of the other person and recognizes the actual possibilities contained therein. If, for instance, an endogenous-depressive

patient discusses with his pastor his sins under which he suffers and his feeling of being lost to God, then it is unwise to try to help him by a suggestive-persuasive attitude. If a married couple has serious, deeply neurotic problems in their marriage, then it would be a mistake to persuade them by a suggestive-pastoral attitude, that if they go to God for help and strength, they will overcome their difficulties. If masturbation has become a problem for someone, it may be questionable to try to persuade him by a suggestive-encouraging attitude that he will be able to stop it. In general, moral or religious strength should not be suggested when actually such a suggestion would be without any foundation. It is even less excusable when in this situation we incorrectly refer to a word of the Bible or prayer.

Persuasion and the Persuasive Element in the Pastoral Conversation

Here again, it is important to distinguish between persuasion as a consistently applied form of psychotherapy and as a possible form of conversation among others, which is used if it seems advisable at a given moment. If it is used in pastoral care then we may speak of the persuasive element in the pastoral conversation. The Genevan physician Dubois objected to suggestive treatment on the ground that the patient was made too dependent on the direct influence of the psychotherapist, without any chance to develop personal self-reliance. In contrast, he pleaded for persuasion in which the cooperation and self-insight of the patient is called upon. The therapist discusses the unreasonableness of the patient's neurotic attitude toward life and, at the same time, appeals to the patient's rational insight into himself. Besides persuasion as an independent psychotherapeutic method, there are other methods in which it takes a more or less important place. This applies, for instance, to individual psychology, which in its psychotherapeutic treatment consists of three distinct phases—the exploring phase, the insight-giving phase, and the reeducational phase. It is especially in the third phase that persuasion is used. One may also recall the logotherapy of Viktor Frankl. I have the impression that in the Netherlands the psychotherapy of many psychiatrists and psychologists consists of a series of conversations with both an analytical and persuasive element.[2]

What they all have in common is the directive function of the therapist who appeals to the rational insight, who tries to give some direction to the psychic or spiritual life, who through all this takes unto himself a reeducational task, and who appeals to the other. In the pastorate persuasion has always had an important place. The pastor often consciously *appeals* to the person. In the biblical word "beseech" this is also implied. This appeal can be very necessary and useful. The Bible itself gives many examples of it. Of course, we should discriminate to what we appeal. It makes a difference whether an appeal is made to somebody's own psychic abilities and strength, his goodwill, or, for instance, to his baptism, to the fact that he is a child of God, to his confirmation.

Special care should be taken with a psychologically uninformed appeal to the *will*. "If you want to, you will be able to do it (or leave it)" is a remark which is often heard in the pastoral conversation, sometimes rightly, sometimes wrongly. The latter does a great deal of harm. The difficulty is often that many people are not able to develop enough willpower. Their will is shut in by lack of freedom, is wrongly directed, is inhibited. Often they do not know what they want. It may be said that with many people,

[2] Refer to my book, *Chapters from Pastoral Psychology*, "Neurosis and Psychotherapy in the Twentieth Century," pp. 77 ff.

especially neurotic people, there is too much of a will (often very cramped) rather than a lack of will. Appealing to their will may have an adverse effect in such a case.

There is another appeal that should be mentioned separately—the appeal to obedience to norms and values or, seen from the gospel, to the commandment of God. It should be remembered that an appeal only works if the values and norms which are at stake have become alive for the other person. In this case I am thinking of ministers, educators, teachers, parents, policemen, who in all sorts of situations in their contact with young people appeal to values and norms which clearly are abracadabra for certain groups of them. Of course, these young people can do nothing else but passively undergo these "sermons," but the result is only a widening of the chasm. The elder person remains the stranger, the remote one, if not the enemy, and what he says—however logical it sounds to the speaker's own ears—seems to come from another planet. The same considerations also apply to a direct religious appeal. In a certain conversation it may be the greatest wisdom, but in another conversation the greatest nonsense, if not still worse, a cruelty. Here I should like to quote Rümke—but it should be remembered that he says this in the first place in regard to psychiatric patients: "One should be very careful with a religious appeal. Sometimes it can be cruel. Often the illness makes it completely impossible to come to a religious experience. Sometimes I make this comparison: If I call someone who is chained to a corner in the room it is cruel and senseless." [3]

Often this apparent "success" and the ultimate failing of this method is seen in certain religious groups, where appeal and persuasion are used extensively. For a short while it looks as if great changes are taking place. But soon the reaction sets in.

[3] *Psychiatrie I*, p. 349.

Clarifying-Interpretative Conversations

By the term "clarifying-interpretative conversations" I mean conversations in which from the pastor's, psychologist's, or physician's side sufficient knowledge of human nature (both intuitive as well as scientific-psychological) and knowledge of human conflicts is required. In this respect I am thinking of conversations which are characterized by an analytic-persuasive approach, in which an especially depth-psychologically oriented discussion of the difficulties and their backgrounds takes place, besides an anagogical or a persuasive stimulating and dynamizing of the person who seeks help. Such clarifying-interpretative conversations frequently constitute the psychotherapeutic method of quite a number of physicians (including psychiatrists), psychologists, and also pastors. Our impression is that the very few predecessors of contemporary pastoral psychology generally used such clarifying-interpretative conversations. We recall the English pastoral psychologist Leslie D. Weatherhead, whose books give an impression of this method, although by using hypnosis and other therapeutic media he often went far beyond the scope of the above mentioned conversations. In the Netherlands J. C. A. Fetter, J. C. Roose and J. G. Fernhout may be mentioned as such predecessors. As far as the authors of this book are concerned, both of us have known a development from the stress laid upon the clarifying-interpretative conversation to the recognition of the significance of counseling. Even today it is probably true that many pastors in their ordinary parish work regularly try to have clarifying-interpretative conversations with their parishioners who have problems, with more or less adequate schooling and training for this work, with more or less success. As these clarifying-interpretative conversations often take place, certainly in the parishes of larger cities, it is well to discuss this in more detail. In the first place, it should be remembered that these conversations are very difficult. If they are carried on in a methodically correct way, then we really are working in the therapeutic field; that is, for the pastor, in the therapeutic phase of the pastoral contact. Then it is necessary to reckon with a number of questions which are important if we are to judge, whether its use is justified. Does the person show enough possibilities for integration? May we count on the ability for psychic assimilation of all that will come up in these conversations? May we assume that there is sufficient growing power to advance through this phase of clarifying-interpretative conversations and with their results? Will the other be able to cope with this process intellectually? Does he honestly wish to be confronted with his own conflicts and problems and to do something about them?

If a series of clarifying-interpretative conversations are decided upon, then it is important to pay attention to the following points:

1. Attention should be paid to the origin and nature of human conflicts and neurotic disturbances. The discussing of certain conflicts or neurotic behavior patterns may be very enlightening. Nevertheless we have to warn against the misunderstanding that sufficient insight alone into the conditioning factors would mean being cured. Someone may have an excellent psychological insight into his own problems of life, without getting one step further.

2. Attention should be paid to the (often deeply suppressed) aggressive feelings of the person, which may play an important part in the originating and continuing of human conflicts. It may happen that someone initially says that he is a man who, however many faults he may have, in any case has no aggressive feelings toward his parents, or wife, colleagues, etc.; while later on during

the conversations it turns out that the man nearly is smothered by his aggressions. Especially in our modern community these things often play an important part. One is not allowed to be aggressive; one should (so it is always said) be kind, adjusted, easygoing in social intercourse, while on the other hand the invitations and incentives to react aggressively in our community are innumerable. It is alarming how much damage is done in human relations and in our personal life by the inwardly unaccepted and unrecognized aggressions. Karen Horney has published excellent studies on this subject.

3. Attention should be paid to the way in which the person experiences his being man or woman in its different aspects and especially in the sexual aspect. Perhaps it is well that the person may freely discuss his sexual difficulties. It may be particularly important that he does not see his sexual difficulties as an isolated part of his life but as an expression in this one particular area of his much more central problems. It may be a relief for the person to become less fixed to his sexual problems as an isolated, and therefore a threatening, hostile area within himself, and to realize that it is an aspect of his personality, of his whole attitude toward life.

4. Attention should be paid to the guilt and guilt feelings which the person mentions, and the effort should be made to develop a differentiated psychological and pastoral approach. Compare what we say in our discussion of confession. (Chap. IX)

5. Attention should be paid to the values and ideals which play a part in the person's life, the extent to which they were introjected, the question of how far they were realized.

6. Attention should be paid to the image which a person has of himself. It is remarkable that, on the one hand, we are impressed time and time again by the fact that people underestimate them-

selves in a harmful way in many respects, but that, on the other hand, we often discover how they believe themselves to be better than they are, that they have an idealized image of themselves, thereby hampering their own authentic development.

7. Attention should be paid to the extent in which a person is able to accept himself adequately. This is a big problem for many. We should learn to realize that in order to make progress we should start with accepting ourselves as we are—that we have to confront ourselves with the sides of ourselves which are difficult to accept: our own failure, our guilt, our sneakiness, and the meanness of which we are guilty, the possibly low and contemptible things that have been done, the narrow and unpleasant aspects of certain acts. The resistance against true self-acceptance can be very tough (and how easy that is to understand).

This form of clarifying-interpretative conversation is often very difficult. The remarks which I have just made are only of use to those who have sufficient knowledge of psychology and, in particular, depth psychology. The physician, psychologist, or minister who is able to carry on these conversations well may be of great help to the person in need. A lot happens during these conversations. Gradually the person gets to know himself better and finds a new start for his life. These conversations have a dynamizing and stimulating influence. It should be remembered that the above is meant for conversations with the essentially not-ill person, who has serious conflicts in his life. Especially in many conflict-psychological and pastoral practices they will occupy a considerable place.

It should be remembered, however, that a merely intellectual interpretation is not only of little value but may be harmful. We should especially be on guard against interpretations resulting from certain preconceived, possibly depth-psychological, schemes and theories. In addition there is the danger that our own problems and conflicts will be projected on the other person. This is something which, in my opinion, happens all too often. It stands to reason that we then get into bigger and bigger transference difficulties. Indeed, even when a series of conversations progresses satisfactorily, transference must be reckoned with. Especially where a longer series of conversations is concerned, this is an important factor and demands our constant attention.

Then, is it actually right that the pastor should carry on conversations in the manner described above? And is there any use to discuss it in such detail? My answer is: We have, whether we like it or not, a situation in which many go to the pastor with more or less serious conflicts (often marital or family problems, but also all sorts of other situations) and expect help from him. It is also clear that numerous pastors respond to it and try to help these people in one or more conversations. In other words, pastors have always conducted these clarifying-interpretative conversations, and it is therefore unavoidable that we study this situation.

Must the pastor do this? I see two possibilities. The first one is that the pastor will *not* do it. I consider this a sensible, legitimate solution. If someone comes to him with problems in which serious emotional conflicts, possibly neurotic factors, are involved, the pastor can say he is prepared to give *pastoral* help but clearly explain that a form of a psychologically more differentiated help is necessary for those difficulties, a psychotherapy which he, the pastor, will not give, either because of lack of time or because he does not consider himself competent or because he does not consider it to be his task. I think it is quite acceptable that a pastor (knowing of the multiplicity of the different forms of help) should not explicitly enter into these too-complicated problems, but explain where and how he sees the limits of his pastoral work. But in that case, the pastor must be consistent and must not let himself be persuaded to discuss the psychic complications which are involved, so that he gets into conversations of a more or less ambivalent character by which no one is helped. I have the impression that this quite often happens. The pastor does not want to refuse if someone appeals for help; he gets into a number of conversations about, for instance, marriage problems, allows himself to be involved in the discussion of the difficult psychic background of the situation, somehow realizes that he doesn't know what to do with it as it gradually becomes evident that all this may lead to a worsening of the situation, even to the breaking up of the marriage, which perhaps could have been saved with more competent help. I think it is important that each pastor set his own limits and discuss them with the person concerned. I know that there are competent pastors who consciously decide against a deeper psychological probing of problems and who are inclined to refer. This, in my opinion, is entirely justified.

The other possibility is that the pastor should give help by such clarifying-interpretative conversations as we have discussed. This is to advance to a therapeutic phase in the pastoral contact, as an extra service which he can offer. But then he has to be capable of it. This demands, besides pastoral wisdom, sufficient psychological knowledge and practical training. It is not necessary to go through complete libraries of psychological literature or to become an allround psychologist; but enough knowledge of twentieth-century psychology to know its understanding of man-in-conflict and the ability to work with it are necessary. I agree with W. A. Smit who in his dissertation pleads for a specific place for this more psychologically skilled pastoral help. However, in my opinion,

131

it is of great importance that a pastor who wants to use this form of help regularly in his ministry shall have done a number of cases under supervision. It may also be wise for the pastor who works with this method to set certain limits to the time he will devote to it. The pastor of an average parish, for instance, might make it a rule to go no further than ten conversations, if only to prevent disturbing the balance of his total program. But it would certainly seem justified for the qualified pastor in such a parish to bring this accent into his work, as other pastors have other accents in their work.

Counseling and Pastoral Counseling

In terms of its derivation the word "counseling" may be traced to the Latin word *"consilium,"* which means "counsel" and may signify both the joint discussion of the problem and its solution. Counseling in general is primarily a conversation between two people about a problem. In that case it is supposed that one is tied up in his problems and is uncertain and doubtful how to cope with them. He expects greater wisdom and better insight, certain guidance, advice from the other person. Thus it is the lack of confidence in his own ability to find an answer, and the hope that discussion will give a satisfactory solution, which will make one go to a counselor.

Within the general meaning of the term, counseling may have a more or less directive character, depending on the agency in whose service the counselor is, as well as the relationship between the counselor and the client. Through the influence of Carl Rogers, however, counseling has developed as an independent psychotherapeutic method (from which we can also learn in all sorts of nontherapeutic relations). In describing this method such terms as "client-centered" and "nondirective" therapy are frequently employed. The central idea of such counseling is self-help as an essential human ability. In this process the relationship which develops between client and therapist is of the greatest importance.

The discussion in previous chapters has made it clear that the premises and methods of counseling not only are important for psychotherapeutic practice, but also for others, who have to carry on conversations with their fellow men in their daily work, amongst whom we think not only of ministers, and social workers, but also of volunteers in all sorts of church work—members of the church council, leaders of young people groups. It will be necessary to discover how, on the one hand, we can gain by this method of conversation, while, on the other hand, we stay with our own specific charge which is implicit in our function—the role which we have in regard to the other person, the aims which have to be realized.

Of course, in other professions conversational situations develop which are different from the psychotherapeutic setting, because this specific conversation as a whole is determined by other, and more, factors than those with which the therapist has to reckon. This brings us to the problem of pastoral counseling. What can the pastor learn from Rogers and other authors in this field? He has, in the first place, the task to lead people to faith and to keep it alive, to help them see themselves in God's light. What matters is that people become disciples of Jesus and live as God's children. For this purpose he administers the word and the sacraments and also carries on conversations. And to do just that does not often turn out to be quite that simple. What we want to keep continuously in mind in this book is the fact that many ministers today are involved in the multiple varieties of the problems of faith and life which modern man knows. There are situations in which the "direct pastoral word" often does not function at all or functions insufficiently. For example, a parishioner can come to his pastor with complicated problems in his marriage. He speaks about his heavy guilt, his ambivalent feelings toward his wife, his feelings of being powerless to change the situation, his inability to pray for this situation, his intention to resign as elder because he no longer can fulfill this task in this situation. Then the pastor can have a conversation in which he seriously and lovingly tells the parishioner about God's forgiveness, makes a number of clarifying remarks about the parishioner's marriage in which he stresses the necessity of continuing to pray, tells him to wait as yet with his request for resignation as elder. Perhaps all that has been said in the conversation is correct, and to a certain extent it is a good pastoral conversation—still, the parishioner concerned may have the feeling, "How is it possible that I can do so little with everything the pastor said tonight?" Also the pastor may have the unsatisfactory feeling, "It was a good conversation, but it is as if the man does not get any further with it." Even if we leave all theory aside for a moment, our daily work forces the question upon us: How can we in the pastorate help the other find his way to overcome the barriers and confusion of his inner life, so that the parishioner concerned can again understand the gospel in its relevance for his life, can again go to communion, can again live more consciously in faith. It is here that the question comes up whether this form of conversation, which in psychotherapeutic counseling finds its own, consistent application, can be of help to us in the ministry. Then the pastor permits a therapeutic phase to enter into the pastoral relation, which as a result takes on the character of counseling in the way described above. Of course, there is a distinct difference between counseling in normal *psychotherapeutic practice* and *pastoral counseling*. In the pastoral conversation we not only take a psychologically continuous process into account, but are also aware of a vertical dimension. Here man discovers a discontinuity in faith which breaks through the psychological categories.

The pastor is the representative of a message which did not originate from men, and which is not to be found within himself but which only can be proclaimed. Revelation and faith are fundamental categories for a pastoral conversation. Pastoral responsibility extends to include concern for what the person will do with his regained freedom (in a psychological sense). Will he want to grow in faith, hope and love? Will he, now that psychic tensions and conflicts are overcome, wish to live as a child of God? The pastor who engages in counseling thus has an aim which differs in quality from the aim of the "neutral" counselor. It may be that he, as pastor, does not have to mention it because the person, through the help of the pastoral counselor, has already found and experienced it. But the pastor never forgets it. For it is his deepest concern that, through his pastoral counseling, the person knows the great pastor Jesus Christ. Unlike the nondirective therapist, the pastor will always keep in mind the significance of God's love and the significance of evangelical guidance—which in fact are two sides of the same thing.

There is one serious objection that is regularly heard when pastoral counseling is discussed. It is the fear that all things will be made relative. Then what about the stability of the Christian faith, the certainty of God's commandments? Is not everything left to man himself? And is it not so, that we must have the courage to call a spade a spade, that we must dare call truth "truth" and sin "sin"? Let us stress it again: If we accept the significance of pastoral counseling, then we surely do not mean to make the certainty of the gospel, the certainty of the Christian faith, or the certainty of God's commandments relative. On the contrary—that which we do make relative is the manner in which all sorts of changing forms of faith and life are made absolute. We are all guilty of that to a much greater extent than most of us realize, even if we are the so-called broad-minded Christians. The way in which we realize our being Christians individually and as a group is a relative matter. If we make it absolute, which often has happened and still happens in church and community, we not only block ourselves but also others and so can damage their souls. We became so used to all we have learned—at confirmation classes and church—that we can no longer stand in awe, and therefore no longer are open to new possibilities and views. We have lost the attitude of the disciples of Christ. This means an impoverishment of our life. It is difficult to tell how many Christians have realized their faith in an anxious, cramped, unworldly manner, and also have denied the existence of certain important aspects of their personality. He who works in pastoral care with such an attitude will always tend to push the other person in certain directions. If the other wants to be a Christian, he has to believe this and do that; in short, he has to accept a specific set of views and patterns for faith and life as absolute directives. Thus he is kept from the freedom of God's children.

In pastoral counseling it is our purpose to help people live in God's light. The pastoral counselor wants to allow the other person the freedom to find his own way, to recognize his own difficulties and to overcome them or to live with them, to discover his own possibilities, to find himself as God intended him to be. In the pastoral conversation we want to create a sphere of confidence, love, and faith in which the other feels called upon by the Gospel and at the same time feels free to respond to it in his own way.

Therefore, I do not believe that there is a conflict between theology and psychology, as is sometimes suggested. Rather, the conflict is between pastoral methods which have to be abolished because the freedom of the gospel and of the Christians are stifled by them and a new, more explicit psychologically oriented method by which a person can be helped to find his own way in religion and to belong to the church in his own personal way.

VII

Psychological Understanding
in Pastoral Counseling

For many centuries the pastor did his work, including pastoral conversation, without ever bothering about the psychological questions which we raise nowadays. He spoke the word with the knowledge that behind it stood another word, the Word of God. He was continually in conversation with the people, and in this conversation he spoke words of encouragement, admonition, consolation, wisdom, joy, peace, suitable to the situation. It cannot be estimated how much good and blessing these words brought in innumerable pastoral conversations in which Christ continued the dialogue with his followers after his departure.

The experience of the twentieth century has been that the pastoral conversation has become a problem in many respects, often for both the parishioner and the pastor. Therefore, it demands special attention. We not only have to deal with the content of the pastoral conversation but also with its form. It is not only a question of what we say to people, but at least as important is the way in which it is said, so that it will really *touch* the other, so that he will *understand* it and be able to do something about it.

But why did a previous generation not know these difficulties, or did they simply solve them in the course of the conversation? Why the explicit attention for these problems in the situation of today? I would suggest that in order to study this problem in more detail we should take a close look at two pastoral conversational situations, which will serve to illustrate that the understanding which is *now* absolutely necessary was superfluous (and furthermore impossible) in earlier days. Next we will examine, in more detail, a third conversation, which will show us how it is possible to find a way in pastoral conversations in our present day practice by using the viewpoints of nondirective counseling.

Pastoral Conversation Yesterday and Today

First of all we will accompany a pastor in a village parish (around 1925) on a home call to a Christian family, the Johnson family, which participates in church life and is a member of a Christian political organization. In this family the religious tradition functions as a matter of course, and their whole way of living is marked by it. All are present. The home call is of set content and form. They all know beforehand which matters will certainly be discussed. There is one particular difficulty which also will be discussed: the twenty-two-year-old daughter has been "going steady" with a young man who does not belong to the church. The pastor stresses once again in a few serious words the dangers of such a situation. It was actually hardly necessary, because the girl herself is already convinced. "Such a thing ought not to be done in Israel." Finally the pastor reads the Bible and says a prayer.

For the most part such a call is appreciated. They converse. They have good contact. They naturally follow the pastoral advice. Why is there a good contact? Because the pastor had intensively studied the psychology of pastoral conversation, because he attended conferences on pastoral care, participated in a clinical training, and maybe had a number of supervised conversations? What silliness! All these things were superfluous and impossible in his world. But this pastor and the people he visits live in the same world, inside of which they understand one another. They share the same religion, the same church, the same political convictions. They have a clear image of what the Christian life should be. They agree on what the minister should be, what may be expected of him, in what spirit he will speak. Furthermore, it is evident that he is not visiting alone, and neither does he find only this family. No, he comes with a numerous company. He has the Bible with him, he brings the prophets and apostles, also the church fathers, the reformers, the Christian political party, the Christian broadcasting company. And as he enters, he finds this same honorable party already here. There is a reciprocal recognition and understanding within the larger context of a close-knit community. What need is there here for the psychology of the pastoral conversation? Of course this home call may be more or less successful. Some problems may crop up with a certain minister which do not occur for others. But they only are fluctuations within a given set context. They remain difficulties within a clearly structured community, misunderstanding within the larger context of a reciprocal understanding and accepting. If the minister who makes the home call is as a person not the most capable and tactful pastor, this will, of course, be noticed. The family will like Reverend Hall better than Reverend Williams at home calls. But it is not a disaster, because Reverend Williams was not alone; he was accompanied by the prophets, the apostles, the church fathers, the reformers, etc., and consequently, there is a mutual understanding. At this home call they have a pastoral conversation and they have good contact. Nobody doubts that it will mean a blessing for all concerned.

In the meantime the world has changed. Let me try to illustrate it by another pastoral conversation from my own pastoral practice in which (as is always done) names and facts are recorded with so many changes that it is impossible to identify the persons involved.

I met Alice A. the first time when she was fifteen. She comes from a simple, strictly religious family. Her father is a surly, difficult person and is active within the church and Christian politics. Because of the dominating manner of the father, there are many difficulties with the children. Alice is continually at odds with him. The mother is a simple, kind woman who is no match for her husband. Alice is artistically inclined and dreams of finding her way in this direction later on. But her father has informed her that he will not accept this. Religion and art cannot go together, in his opinion. In religious and church matters the children are pressed, if not compelled, to participate. Alice goes to church reluctantly and attends my confirmation classes with great resistance. I was able to establish a good relationship with her, and had several conversations with her between the ages of fifteen and eighteen. At the age of eighteen she was confirmed in another city because the family had moved there. After that I lost sight of her. After eight years (she is then twenty-six years old and has been able to follow her ambition in spite of her father's protests) I accidentally met her. After some hesitation she suddenly asked whether I could receive her sometime. She would like to talk about the years just past. Here is a short summary of what she told me in the ensuing conversation.

Strange that I come back to you even though you are a minister, because I don't feel I belong to a church at all anymore. When I think of church, or when I go there on very rare occasions, then I am often reminded of how father wanted to force religion upon us and of all the quarreling this caused. Besides, what does he make of it himself? I think that many parents are hypocrites, with pious words, but their own behavior. . . . In any case, religion means little or nothing to me anymore. All these theological terms and expressions have become only abstractions for me. It doesn't mean anything to me, it doesn't really touch me, and what use is it then to me? I find the church and the church services hopelessly old-fashioned. For the rest, I can't experience religion with my heart at a fixed hour, even though I still have faith. And then the authority which so many ministers and clergy usurp. They always have the right answer to everything, and always know why people who think differently are wrong. I think it is so terribly complicated to know what to think about the questions of faith, behavior, life and death. There are so many different opinions which all make some impression on me. Sometimes I prefer this and at other times something else. In certain situations you would want to be a Christian, but in other situations you can't do anything with it. Everything is so relative, even the values and norms in which you believe. Because of that I don't bother too much about it and feel happy with it. I make a good living, I enjoy everything wholeheartedly, I love to feel the wind sweeping past my ears when in a car or on a scooter, I love the country and also the city where so much is to be enjoyed. I must admit that to a certain extent I find little or no time for myself. For that I am too busy. Also, because of that, everything concerning religion has fallen outside my interest. Furthermore, in my present circle of friends practically no one believes, and that also influences my own behavior. And all those friends manage without faith and church. There are very gifted people amongst them, even academically trained people, for whom Christian faith does not mean anything either. Sometimes I think that as people can do more and acquire more certainties and science progresses, faith diminishes. Is faith maybe a wish or dream

142

after all? Is God maybe a father-projection? Of course, things aren't as easy for me as people who only know me on the surface may think and as it probably often seems. After I left home and lived by myself in rooms, things were very difficult for me at first. Often I felt very lonely. This has changed because of my job and my many friends. Furthermore, I met someone so that I wasn't lonely anymore. He is much older than I am. In addition, he is married. That was a miserable situation, because I was friends with both of them. Sometimes I feel rotten toward her. I took away her husband. But why should he and I not have the right to happiness if we love each other? Again something for which people in the church have no understanding. But I must honestly admit that because of all this, I often feel miserable. Sometimes I can well understand the atmosphere in the books of Françoise Sagan because I myself recognize something of the feelings and experiences which are described there. Otherwise, I loathe these books. Strange, actually, that I was confirmed. I was only eighteen—but I had such good contact with you, which was also an important factor. Now I sometimes regret it. Often I think I don't believe anymore, but sometimes I also long for God, especially now that the divorce will become official, and we will get married. I often worry about these things, sometimes I wish I could pray.

This extensive effusion which I have recorded in a more orderly manner, was the starting point for a number of conversations which we will not discuss further. What we are interested in is to get to know the situation with which we are now confronted. What can we say about this situation compared with the previous one? I would like to call attention to several points.

1. The pastor did not enter into the house of his parishioner where he would find the family gathered together as a small church within the church. On the contrary, if there is one place where the pastoral conversation with Alice would be a complete failure, it would be there. We won't get any contact with Alice within

the family (this also was true when she still lived at home) but we will in the quiet sphere of the personal pastoral conversation in the office of the pastor, which to her is as a safe harbor.

2. When we entered into the Johnson's home we knew whom we would find there—the Johnsons in the first place, but around and behind them would be the prophets and the apostles, the church fathers and the reformers, the reformed synod, and the village community. But when Alice enters our office, a very remarkable and colorful company comes with her. Maybe for some pastors it brings the association "Samson, the Philistines be upon thee!" Anyway, you find in her company also the prophets, the apostles, the church fathers, the reformers—but she is at odds with them in different degrees. They have, as a matter of fact, more or less lost their importance. In her immediate company you will find quite different persons, Sigmund Freud, D. H. Lawrence, Françoise Sagan—just to name a few of the divergent people who have influenced her by their publications. She enters with tousled hair, because she had just raced in on her scooter, and in her mind are still fragments of conversations with her friends she has just left and who agree with one another on very little—except on one thing, that God does not exist. Amongst these friends, as the most important, is the married older man, who wants to make her understand that if people love each other, everything is permitted, and that it is hypocritical to think differently and to want to tie the pure feelings of people toward each other down to strict rules. That is the company with which Alice enters and which will be involved in the conversation. And here is the pastor: In his company there are the prophets, the apostles, the church fathers, the reformers and quite a number of other persons, partly, indeed, the persons with whom Alice arrived—But their relationship in regard to one another is somewhat different than their arrangement

around Alice. And there are also a number of psychologists with whom he has become acquainted. In any case, it is immediately clear that we now have a completely different situation than at the home call at the Johnsons. Whether we get real contact in this conversation depends on a lot of factors. A very small detail is enough to make the conversation one in which we talk at cross purposes, a hopeless conversation. Then this conversation may be the last that Alice will have with a minister. Let us realize what she expects based on what we know of her life history and on what she told us in the first part of the conversation about her situation and opinions.

a. She expects that she will be allowed to talk freely and will be taken seriously, even though what she thinks may be diametrically opposed to the viewpoint of the pastor.

b. She expects also that all the others whom she brings with her and who play an important part in her life will be taken seriously as well.

c. She does not expect clear and short pastoral advice, but expects to find someone who accepts her independence and who perhaps can help her in one way or another to find her way.

d. She expects to have a conversation with someone, not primarily because he is a minister, but because she trusts him, and also because it will be useful to talk with him about her problems.

e. She expects, in spite of her ambivalence in this respect, that this man will be able to help her see things more in God's light. She expects that after all he will be a *pastor*. This pastor is confronted with an extremely difficult but also a fascinating and important task. He will be wise not to read only the Bible, the church fathers, the reformers, not only to stand open and listening in the world of today, but also to study intensively the psychology of pastoral conversation. For his colleague of the previous example this would have been nonsense, and also an impossibility; the discipline we call pastoral psychology did not exist! And rightly so!

We have tried to describe pastoral conversation in entirely different situations. We have chosen very different situations on purpose. Many cases in which we get involved will probably be less extreme. But in any case we can say that pastoral conversation presents us with very many problems in our changed and changing world because today the situations which we meet are infinitely variegated. When starting a pastoral conversation, we have to reckon with numerous uncertain and unknown factors, so that time and time again it is an adventure to make a contact and to hold a conversation in this particularly concrete situation. With all this it is also evident that the emotional relationship between the pastor and the Johnsons was determined by the set role which the pastor had in the world of his parishioners. The emotional relationship between the pastor and the other person in our present-day community is much less stable. In any meeting it will need to be discovered and recognized and later on probably corrected. But in any case, close attention to the emotional relationship is demanded of the modern pastor, for it is of basic importance for successful conversation, and it is no longer sustained on both sides by a network of common understanding.[1]

The Case of Wilma B.

After these illustrations of pastoral practice, we will now proceed with a detailed recording and discussion of a conversation in which it is clearly demonstrated that the nondirective method can

[1] The greater part of the above, especially the examples, also appeared with some revisions in my article, "Gesprek en Contact" (Conversation and Contact), *Bezinning*, XV, No. 5, 256-71.

be most useful for the minister in a situation in which a serious conflict is presented to the pastor. This is the case of Wilma B.

Mrs. B. from The Hague calls by telephone and urgently requests an appointment with the pastor. When she comes she has the following story. Her eldest, the twenty-three-year-old daughter of the family of four has been going steady for six months with a twenty-eight-year-old Roman Catholic young man. The girl attends Roman Catholic confirmation classes and is contemplating becoming Roman Catholic herself. Mrs. B. and her husband—they consider themselves Protestant, but do not participate—are dead set against their daughter becoming a Roman Catholic as well as marrying a Roman Catholic. Furthermore, they are of the opinion that the young man in question has an unstable social position, and they are worried about the future for this reason. They will not give their consent to this marriage. In the meantime the young couple have definitely decided to get married anyway. In a few months the wedding will take place. Wilma had received no religious education but tried to find her own way in this respect. She had attended a few church services of this pastor for a brief period and her reaction to these gave Mrs. B. the hope that her daughter might be prepared to talk with him. The pastor tells Mrs. B. that this would be possible only if Wilma herself would want to do this, asks her to tell her daughter about her going to him (she went without informing Wilma), and writes a letter to Wilma in which he refers to the conversation with her mother and tells her that he will receive her if she would like to discuss the situation. When she comes, the following conversation takes place after the exchange of greetings.

Pastor: You know the background of our conversation, the fact that your mother called on me. Apparently you yourself are also prepared to have a talk. Maybe you can tell something about the situation in so far as you think it useful.

Wilma: Yes, to tell the truth, I myself had intended to call you. Actually, it is strange that Mam, after all, established the contact! That is probably because I told her that I had attended your church service a few times. Anyway, I myself felt the need to discuss the situation. . . . Yes, things are very difficult. [short pause, then in a sudden outburst] Why does Mam always want to tell me what to do? Why can't I make my own decisions? I should know whether I want to become Roman Catholic or anything else. And I'll decide for myself whom I will marry! Mam doesn't have to decide everything for me.

Pastor: It makes you furious that your mother does not give you the freedom to find your own way.

Wilma: Right. Honestly, I have never realized that I could hate her because of this. Oh, of course she means well, but she always has laid down the law to me. But I won't take it any longer! I will choose my own husband if I want to get married and join the church which I choose.

Pastor: You have definitely decided to make your own decisions and no longer be told what to do.

Wilma: Yes, you know for some years I have been wanting to leave home and take rooms. I felt it would be a lot better for myself and the whole situation at home. I had the feeling that I could not become the person I would want to be if I stayed with my parents. Tensions and clashes were every-day occurrences. But do you think my parents would let me? "You won't find a better place to stay anywhere else," they tell me, and then: "What would people say if you were to take rooms in the same city where your parents live? You can't bring this shame on us." But I have had enough of it. I want to leave, I want my freedom!

Pastor: You feel your central problem is that you want to live your own life and do not get the chance for this if you stay at home.

Wilma: Yes, you know I am sure that Mam and Dad love me, but they understand so little. Sometimes Mam and I can get along well. [She then tells in more detail about the relationship with her parents and its difficulties. At a given moment the conversation continues as follows.]

Wilma: [She is speaking much more quietly now than in the previous parts where she was vehement and emotional.] I also believe that then [when she would no longer be at home] I would be able to think about my engagement and the question of whether or not I would want to become a Roman Catholic.

Pastor: You have the feeling that you do not have the right climate now to come to a responsible decision.

Wilma: Indeed, Mam and Dad are all at once such good Protestants and are so critical of the Roman Catholic Church. I can't stand this. Just as if Roman Catholics can't be good Christians. I hate this anti-Roman Catholic attitude of Mam. . . . But what I want myself, I really don't know . . . I don't know. I have little religious education, and I probably would have become Protestant if I had not met Henry. He and I attend the Roman Catholic Church regularly, and I attend some kind of confirmation class. There is much in the Roman Catholic Church that fascinates me. . . . But anyway, I don't want any interference from Mam in this.

Pastor: You find it unacceptable that your parents want to lay down the law to you in this respect, but for yourself you feel that you cannot as yet see all the aspects of the situation and that you still have to discover your own way.

Wilma: Right, and that is the way it is with Henry, too. To tell the truth —when I sometimes try to think quietly about the situation, then I am not at all sure about it, whether we actually do match well. Henry says that he is quite sure, and he wants to get married soon. When I tried to discuss our marriage with my parents, they were immediately furiously against it and refused to consent. My God! What a session that was! And then I thought: But now you will know that the time has past in which you can tell me what to do. And then all at once things went very fast— and within two months we will be married. . . . [Pause] Actually, I would have preferred to have waited to be more sure. . . . Henry was so insistent . . . too insistent, I sometimes think.

Pastor: You feel that because of your parents' attitude and Henry's insistence everything developed very rapidly, but that you yourself are still somewhat uncertain about your coming marriage.

Wilma: Yes, do you know, sometimes Henry has so little consideration for me. If he thinks that we love each other enough and that we are to be married in April, then this *must* happen, and he refuses to understand that it is different with me. This can make me furious sometimes. Don't I have the right to experience it in my own way?

Pastor: You feel that Henry does not give you enough room to develop freely in this matter and you resent that very much.

Wilma: Yes . . . sometimes I think: Am I crazy to step from one cage into the other? . . . I first want to have time to think about it. . . . To-night, I will simply tell my parents that I will take rooms. I am not going to ask, I won't ask Henry, I will only tell them and then see what happens.

Pastor: You now see what you want to do in the first place. [Pause] If you would like to discuss it further one of these days, you may call me.

After a week Wilma comes back. She is clearly relaxed and re-lieved. The evening of the previous conversation, she told her parents she would look for rooms. As early as the next day she found a room and the day after that she moved there. She is very happy to have taken this step. In this conversation she is occupied with her impending marriage and her ambivalence toward Henry.

Four days later she comes back for a third conversation. She tells the pastor that she has postponed the marriage for an in-definite time, will not see Henry for two months, does not want to see the pastor for the time being. She has discontinued the Roman Catholic confirmation classes, and she will go on a fort-night's holiday with a girl friend.

After two months she comes back. After that the pastor has another two conversations with her. The engagement has been definitely broken. She goes to her parents regularly. She has a much better relationship with them than before, and with her approval the pastor has had a clarifying conversation with them. She attends confirmation classes in the city where she lives. Later on she became a member of a Protestant church and married a Protestant partner.

Of the five conversations which the pastor had with her, four were strictly nondirective. In the fifth conversation, when she brought it up, they discussed her attitude towards religion; information and instructions were given, and the pastor referred her to a minister in her own city.

Dangers and Risks in Wilma's Case

The above case is one which presented the possibility of all sorts of difficulties for the pastor in his contact with the situation. We shall have a closer look at it.

Mrs. B. seeks contact with the pastor without consulting her daughter. She hopes to make him an ally in her assumption that a minister, when he is confronted with such a case, will only see one task: To come to the aid of the threatened Protestant fortress, and to keep the girl from going to the Roman Catholic Church. Therefore she stresses this side of the matter: Our Protestant daughter wants to become Roman Catholic. What do you say about that, Reverend?

There are a few things which the pastor notices for himself in the conversation:

1. This woman is a very dominating person in the family.

2. Her actual concern is not the possible religious decision of her daughter, but that she considers the future husband simply unacceptable both as a person and because of his social position.

3. Generally, this woman will find it difficult to let her daughter live her own life.

It usually means a very unfortunate start for a pastoral contact if it is to take place through the initiative of someone who is in conflict with the person with whom the conversations will be held. Usually, I don't do it. If either of the parents or the husband or wife comes to discuss his conflicts with his child or partner, without the other person concerned knowing of it, and asks that I contact the other person, I usually refuse. For it should be realized that such a person often *means* to engage the pastor as an "ally"! But exception should be made to the above rule if there is good reason for it. It was evident that in this case, while there were great difficulties and even dangers, the mother thought, based on what her daughter had told her, that she could expect that her daughter would agree to a contact with *this* pastor. But then the condition should be: "Put all cards on the table. Tell your daughter that you contacted me without consulting her!" And from the side of the pastor, a proposition which she can feel completely free to accept or not.

Wilma comes. About what will the conversation be? About the fact that a good Protestant does not become Roman Catholic and does not bring this disgrace upon her parents? That is what the mother expects. The pastor is probably inclined to think that he is once again confronted with one of those difficult cases of an impending mixed marriage. He will present all possible points of view which are involved with wisdom and tact, to convince the girl of the dubious character of her plans. Let us try to think how such a conversation might start.

Pastor: You know that your mother told me about the difficulties of the situation, and I am glad that you have come to talk about it. You know, my experience as pastor is that people often don't realize what is involved in a mixed marriage or in becoming a Roman Catholic, and because of that it may be important that it be discussed. Really, it should not be underestimated how deeply it will influence your life—the marriage of a Protestant to a Roman Catholic, or the possible conversion of Protestant to Roman Catholic.

Actually this beginning does not look unpleasant at all; the pastor wants to get to the heart of the matter without any detours, and he tries to point to this central problem. Nonetheless this is a dangerous start. Firstly, this opening sentence may give Wilma the impression that the pastor objectively accepts, without any doubt, her mother's version as being correct (so that she immediately experiences him as having taken her mother's side). Next, he accepts the fact that the central problem is simply that of a mixed marriage, possibly the difficulty of a Protestant who is considering an important decision—conversion to the Roman Catholic Church. That which follows shows that matters lie quite differently. Finally, Wilma can easily, from his words, get the impression, "Oh, again someone who knows better than I do and who will tell me what to do!" What would have followed if the pastor had started the conversation as we just suggested? We could imagine the following:

Wilma: I understand, Reverend, that Mam did inform you fully! And let me immediately answer you that Henry and I certaintly are aware of those matters and know what we want. Of course, I understand that this is an important matter. But I know quite well what I must do. Mam doesn't have to tell me and—I hope you don't mind me saying so—neither do I need a minister to tell me what to do.

With this has happened what we could have expected when the pastor started as indicated above. The authority conflict in which Wilma is entangled she immediately transfers to her contact with

153

the pastor. Again she meets someone who "knows better" and who will tell her. She reacts accordingly. That she doesn't do justice to this kind pastor does not matter as far as her personal feelings about the situation are concerned. It is clear that this conversation will come to a dead end. Let us for a while imagine how things could continue in the given conversational situation.

Pastor: But, of course, Miss B., you don't need a pastor who will make decisions for you. It stands to reason that I respect and accept your personal freedom completely. But I do wonder whether you really sufficiently know and realize the consequences of these things. Assuming that you want to remain Protestant, do you really know what the Roman Catholic church asks of you as a condition for your marriage? Or assuming that you yourself will become Roman Catholic, have you really sufficiently realized what a big—in my opinion, unbridgeable—chasm there is between the Roman Catholic Church and the Reformed Church, and that you have to accept all sorts of human opinions and unbiblical practices?

What will Wilma think and feel hearing such an argumentation? I think something such as: He says that he respects my personal freedom, but actually he does not! He keeps on forcing his opinions upon me. He thinks he knows better than I do—just like mother! He does want to push in a certain direction—just like mother! Of course, Wilma feels threatened. She is strengthened in her resistance. She becomes more and more aggressive—even though she behaves correctly during the conversation. She may say: All right, you say so, but I believe that if you really love each other, the Protestant can sacrifice enough to sign those conditions. After all, you marry another Christian. And doesn't the Reformed Church have its own human viewpoints and unbiblical practices, too? Isn't it conceited to reproach only the other party?

We could imagine that the pastor would turn the conversation to the contents and consequences of the conditions of dispensation in the Roman Catholic Church, or that he brings up Mariology, or the doctrine of transsubstantiation, to clarify the—in his opinion, unbridgeable—chasm between Rome and the Reformation. But one thing is certain: it is a hopeless conversation. They are talking at cross purposes. The pastor will at the end have the feeling: "Quite a nice girl, but she is stubborn and obstinate; she won't listen. And how little she understands." One thing the pastor has certainly brought about. Wilma will leave with the feeling: "My parents won't get their way, even though they seek the help of a thousand pastors!" The result of the pastor's effort was that the marriage will take place. A fatal result of a well-meant pastoral conversation! This will show that the pastoral conversation always leads to "something," either good or bad. It often brings about a change in the situation. It plays a part in the taking of decisions. Because of that, to hold pastoral conversations is a privilege but also a precarious matter. Through the pastoral conversation, we can lead someone to faith or block his way to it. Through a pastoral conversation we can save a marriage and family or cause its dissolution. Because of that, everything that is humanly possible should be done so that we will be able to meet the challenge of this work.

A Skillful Use of Pastoral Counseling

Actually the conversation had a different development than we have just assumed. What the pastor really did in the first sentences was to shortly refer to the motive for this conversation (mother's initiative) and then immediately let Wilma explain the problem herself: "Maybe you yourself can tell something about the situation

155

in so far as you think it useful?" Nothing gives Wilma the impression "Oh, he already thinks he knows how matters stand because mother told him." Here she is simply offered a relationship in which, if she wishes, she can talk about those things which are important to her and as she experiences them. Here should be remembered again the importance of the tone of voice in which this is said. The reader may try to say this first sentence in a somewhat stern, threatening (possibly also in a somewhat cynical and sarcastic) manner, sounding like: Now let's see whether this obstinate young lady, who wants to become Roman Catholic because of her sweetheart, thinks she can justify her attitude; and after that, speak in a kind, accepting manner, which invites further communication. Then he will feel that the contact is immediately broken with the first sentence (even though the conversation will go on for a short while), and that in the second case the way is opened to continue.

We now make a remarkable discovery: Wilma remarks that she herself had also considered seeking contact with the pastor. . . . Pause. . . . Then suddenly an emotional outburst, "Why does Mam always have to tell me what to do?"

When Wilma has finished speaking, there is a big temptation for the pastor. He may think and also say: "Yes, I quite well understand that you resent the interference of your parents and that you revolt against it. This is human. But the heart of the matter still is your impending mixed marriage, your possible conversion to the Roman Catholic Church. We will have to give our attention to these problems, because it concerns your future. Let us, therefore, forget about mere accidents and understandable human reactions and return to the matter itself." All this would have been wisely thought and said, but the capital objection is that the pastor then would demonstrate that he does not know how to listen, that he cannot enter into the other person's situation, that he does not try here to get to know her frame of reference and think with her, but assumes that he understands her problems better than she does, and that she should accept from him the nature of the central problem.

Actually, the pastor said in this conversation after this vehement aggressive outburst against the mother: "It makes you *furious* (and in the manner of speaking the emotion should be echoed) that your mother does not give you the freedom to find your own way!" In other words, the pastor says: "If I understand the pent-up feeling which you have—if based on what you say and how you say it, I try to feel with you what matters to you—if I, in the confusion of thoughts and emotions and in the tension with which you live at the moment, try to be with you as much as possible, then you feel in the multiplicity of problems at this moment the central problem to be that "It makes me furious that Mam does not give me the freedom to find my own way." Wilma reacts with an emphatic "Right." She feels she has been recognized. All at once there is someone who is not going to talk about the contrast between Roman Catholic and Protestant, who does not stress the objections of a mixed marriage, who does not point out that the social stability of her fiancé may be questionable, who does not point out that a daughter may not express herself so aggressively about her mother, but gives her the feeling that he is prepared to accompany her in the reconnaissance of her situation. She can now continue to become conscious of the pressure which her dominating mother exercised in her life, her increasing feeling of resistance and protest which now culminate in the present situation in which the conflict threatens to be fought out in a particularly unpalatable and turbid manner in connection with central life decisions: religion and marriage.

"I choose my husband if I want to be get married, and go to the church I choose." Again this is a dangerous point in the situation, especially if it is a pastor who knows something (or perhaps a lot) about psychology. He, of course, has already noticed what dangers threaten: A girl who, in a turbulent authority conflict with her parents (especially her mother), forces life decisions which are not justified. She obviously lacks the inner freedom to come to mature decisions. Faith and love are involved in an alarming manner in her conflict with her mother. It is quite understandable that the pastor believes he has a clear psychological insight into the situation and says this to her. This is a much used method which, in my opinion, is unnecessarily dangerous in this case. The pastor could say something such as, "Yes, I'm beginning to understand the situation. But don't you realize that under the influence of your mother you may easily come to decisions which you may regret later on?" The risk of this interpretative-diagnostic answer is that Wilma, after all, will experience the pastor as someone who knows better than she does and who judges her from that standpoint— and how sensitive she is to that! Then she could say: "Yes, I know quite well what you mean, but you don't have to think that Henry and I do not know what we want. You better leave that to us." And the pastor may answer: "Yes, I understand that you put it this way, but experience has taught me that often it is difficult for a person to know himself in such a situation." And so the discussion may continue.

In addition, the pastor cannot be *absolutely sure* that her decisions (in spite of the disturbing factors) could not be the *right* decisions. He may feel very alarmed about what he has heard, but nonetheless it would not be right to think: "Oh, I already know how matters are." Therefore, it is not only *safer* but also *better* to continue in the same way and to reflect Wilma's thoughts and feel-

ings. "You have definitely decided to make your own decisions."
—Wilma feels free to further probe into her conflicts, to which
the pastor answers with the summarizing empathical reflection:
"You feel your central problem is that you want to live your own
life and do not get the chance for this if you stay at home." Next
there is a phase in the conversation in which Wilma talks about
the tension between her and her parents and only then returns
(now more quietly) to the problem of her impending marriage
and conversion to the Roman Catholic Church. We will not discuss
the remainder of the conversation in such a detailed fashion. But
we notice that now that she has been confronted with the central
problem more consciously, she can also think more freely and in a
more relaxed manner about her fiancé and her faith. She becomes
aware of her own uncertainties, becomes more conscious of her
ambivalent feelings towards Henry (but how different is this
compared to a psychological interpretation by the pastor!) and
finally concludes that she needs time to gain clearer insight into
the matter. Then there is a long silence—a silence in which quite
a few things happen, because she ends the conversation by com-
municating her decision: "I am going to take rooms."—This to
her means: "I want room and freedom to be myself." What happens further has been shortly discussed above.

Final Considerations About the Case of Wilma B.

There are some additional aspects of the case of Wilma B. which
should be considered.

In the first place, I would point out the importance of the relationship between the pastor and Wilma as it was before she entered
his office. This is, of course, important. In the case of the ordinary

psychotherapist, it may often happen that a client enters who perhaps was referred by someone else and probably feels quite neutral personally toward this psychotherapist. That is usually not the case if someone comes to speak with the pastor about his personal problems. There already *is* a certain relationship, if not of a personal nature, than perhaps that of minister-churchgoer, minister-confirmation candidate, etc. Or he has read an article by the pastor which impressed him, so that there already exists a certain relationship. In Wilma's case the precounseling relationship has a negative aspect (Mother tried to get the pastor as her ally, without consulting Wilma, so that the conversation can become more difficult, if not impossible) and a positive side (Wilma happened to attend the pastor's church services twice and was touched by certain things he said). This gives her enough confidence, so that her mother's action in this case had no harmful effects.

As pastor, one must realize that preaching can open or close the way to the personal pastoral conversation. If a pastor preaches about Zacchaeus, he may, however much he stresses the fact that Jesus accepted this publican, talk about Zacchaeus as a collaborator, a traitor, etc. in a negative, cynical, malicious manner; then the ex-Nazi in the church will not easily come to this pastor when in trouble. And about the history of David and Bathsheba some pastors can preach in a manner which discourages anyone who ever committed adultery from going to this pastor to tell of his difficulties. This has nothing to do with the question of whether sin may not be called sin. It deals with the question of the extent to which the pastor loves the sinner (the fellow sinner) with the love of Christ.

It would also be instructive to ask what happens in the course of these conversations. What is the situation Wilma finds herself in? It is obvious that she does not quite know herself. She is engaged to a Roman Catholic young man and attends Roman Catholic confirmation classes. She rebels against her parents who will not let her find her own way. But she herself is not clearly aware that under these circumstances she is in danger of being pushed (without really wanting it) in a certain direction, even though she has been saying during the last few weeks that she does know what she wants. In other words, there is confusion within herself, also a powerlessness, an emotionally motivated lack of freedom to make decisions. She is unable to disassociate herself from her problems.

Which emotions come up? How does she experience her relationship with the pastor? To start with the latter, she apparently experiences this relationship as one in which no one wants to tell her or to force her to do something, but in which she feels she is invited to be herself without restraint. This implies the freedom to vent her pent-up emotions, which she soon does wholeheartedly. It is amazing how soon she then gets to the heart of the matter. What happens in and with her is the following:

1. She all at once becomes aware of the repressed side of her personality, particularly in regard to her mother and her fiancé.

2. She gains distance from her problems and becomes more relaxed.

3. A better integration becomes possible. Out of the confusion she finds her way to a better insight into her problems with which she can do something.

4. All this gives her more self-confidence and makes a provisional decision possible.

5. Through that she becomes more like the young woman she wants to be (compare: "I have the feeling that I never could become the person I want to be if I were to stay with my parents.")

Perhaps it should be pointed out that Wilma's case is not really representative of the mixed engagements and marriages with which the pastor may become involved. It is not meant as such. It is an illustration of the necessity first to listen patiently, to listen with empathy for a long time, before the pastor can think that he knows the real problem. I also believe that the complicating and confusing influences, which result from all sorts of conflict situations, play a much greater part than often is thought. Quite a few mixed marriages probably would not have taken place if parents and clergy had not worked against them so fervently.

But of course, the impending mixed marriage often requires a much more direct approach. Such an example we see in the case of Dick H. who comes to the office of the pastor and says that he has been going steady with a Roman Catholic girl for half a year. They love each other, and both think that they need no longer wait to form a clearer picture of the possible consequences of a continued relationship. Dick tells it as follows:

"We love each other. We agree about that. Because of that, we will do our best to find a solution so that we can get married in spite of the big differences between the churches. We have often discussed religion together, and I believe that today we not only accept each other as Christians but that we also experience our faith together, for instance, in prayer. We believe that if you love each other and also know yourselves to be joined by faith, there must be a possibility to find a way together. But now the difficulty is that neither of us knows enough about the standpoints and conditions as they are now in the Roman Catholic and Protestant churches. As long as you haven't anything to do with it, you don't investigate it in detail. Therefore we would first of all like to know what we are up against. Could you give me some more information on this?"

The reader realizes that at this point we have to abandon the non-directive method. Dick does not present emotional difficulties which he does not understand. Clarification by reflection or something like that is useless. If we would do it, it would be ridiculous. Just imagine the pastor who would reply to Dick's last words: "You feel as if you do not know enough about the standpoints of the church, and you would like to hear them from me."

Dick would have been most astonished: "What is the matter with him! That is what I asked him." Generally we may say that the person who reflects at the right moment will discover that his words will further the development of thoughts and feelings of the other person. Something *happens*. A reflective answer which is out of place, as described here, blocks the conversation. Nothing will happen anymore. Here the pastor only has to say how matters stand. He must inform Dick as honestly and objectively as possible. Dick learns much that neither he nor his fiancée knew concerning the mixed marriage. When he leaves he is downhearted. "We will discuss it together."

Dick and his girl friend have discussed it a lot together. They have also spoken with a priest. After a few months Dick comes back for another conversation. They have already come to a decision: They have broken up.

"We didn't see any way out after all. We both think it is awful. We have come to this conclusion: the rules of the church which form a barrier are not according to God's will. Nell and I are both convinced that the conditions of the Roman Catholic Church for possible dispensation cannot be justified from an evangelical point of view. But because we do not want to break with the church, we see no other possibility but to break up."

In this case the problems in connection with the mixed marriage are quite different from the case of Wilma. Here it concerns two young people who love each other, who take their belonging to their respective churches seriously, who ask the pastor for information and based on that work together on their problems and finally come to the above-mentioned conclusion. Sad and indignant about the pastoral guidance of the church, they decide in spite of that to stay with their church community and to break up.

Another remark—with Wilma we have a psychically healthy and well-integrated girl, who gets into a serious conflict situation in which she threatens to take dangerous steps. As soon as she is helped adequately, she rapidly finds the way to help herself come to a clearer insight into herself and takes important decisions. Should Wilma have developed much more in neurotic directions because of the difficulties in the parent-child relationship, then such a rapid reorientation would not have been possible.

Finally, the case of Wilma is a typical example of *pastoral counseling*. The pastor discovers by listening empathically and understandingly that he is dealing with a psychic conflict situation which hinders Wilma from coming to a clear insight into her problems. That is why he reacts immediately by giving room to a therapeutic phase in that relationship and temporarily works as a counselor. But at the same time, it is a typical example of *pastoral* counseling. This relationship had already been established by the dialogue which originated between Wilma and the pastor in the church service, by way of the sermon, before there was any personal contact. But it is especially *pastoral* counseling because the contact does not come to an end at the moment that Wilma is freed of her psychic problems and can orientate herself more freely. That is generally the end of the *psychiatrist-client* relationship. For the *pastor* there is a final *pastoral* phase. In Wilma's case it appeared in the fifth and last conversation (but now in a new way) when the question arose as to how she, who had received no guidance in religion from her parents, would find her way to faith—a question which also occupied her long before she knew Henry. This conversation ended with a referral to confirmation classes which resulted in her becoming a member of the church. To those who ask whether this fifth conversation could not have been held the first time, and whether this long roundabout way of four nondirective conversations was necessary (Pastor, how can you justify this in regard to your parish), I would answer that, after all, each pastor is free to "go straight to the point." I am afraid (as I said at the beginning) that afterward his conclusion would be: "There was no talking to this girl. In spite of everything, she wanted to carry through with the marriage." And he probably would be right. But then in a different way than he himself meant.

VIII

Unique Dimensions of the Pastoral Conversation

Implicit in this book from its very beginning has been the assumption that the pastoral conversation is not simply a replica of other conversations, but that it has certain unique dimensions which clearly differentiate it from other conversations. The effort to identify these points of difference has engaged my attention during several years, both as a student and as a teacher of the psychology of conversation. I have attended discussions on this subject at several conferences and meetings and, besides that, have often discussed it personally. In particular, I should like to recall the intensive study in the Commission of Pastoral Care of the Dutch Reformed Church, to which I am greatly indebted. In all these discussions it became more and more evident how difficult it is to define the specific nature of the pastoral conversation accurately.

A Comparison with Other
Conversational Situations

Perhaps, as an introduction, it will be well to ask first what is
peculiar to the conversational situation in some other professions
where care for our fellow men is also very important, so that we
will have some material for comparison.

It is apparent that the conversational situation of *physician-pa-
tient* is determined by the being ill or feeling ill of the patient, who
expects to be cured by the physician. The *psychiatrist-patient* relationship seems to me to be a special instance of this, comparable
to that in the other medical specialties. We will not attempt to ask
how it is in those cases in which the not-ill person turns to the
psychiatrist with his conflicts. It is well known that there is no
agreement about this amongst psychiatrists. Besides those who consider the conflicts of the healthy person as their field of action,
there are others who reject it, because then, in their opinion, the
psychiatrist no longer works as physician but enters the field of
the pastor, the psychologist, the pedagogue, the social worker, anyway, he leaves the sphere of medical science. Next let us consider
the *social-worker-client* conversational situation. Here it is evident
that the policies of the particular agency are a decisive factor. The
conversation is determined by the different objectives. That which
joins all social workers is the fact that they are confronted with
problems which have social as well as psychological aspects within
the limits of the given objectives.

Another modern profession is that of the practicing psychologist.
The *psychologist-client* conversational situation is determined by
the objective of their contact (compare, for instance, the voca-
tional counselor, the psychotherapist, etc.). It always concerns
service to others—at their request—based on the insights of psychic

167

relationships, based on psychological expert knowledge. These few brief remarks about the conversational situation in some other professions have already made it apparent that it is difficult to determine the specific nature of the pastoral interview more concisely. One thing is evident—the specific nature can certainly not be found in the *subject* of the conversation, for instance, by saying that in the pastoral interview (only) theological questions and so-called "religious matters" are brought up for discussion. On the contrary, it is the experience of pastors that, if they are completely open-minded, people will discuss all sorts of problems, with which they are confronted in life, with them. This has been noted throughout this book, and we have continually seen it confirmed in our conversations with pastoral workers.

European Discussion of the Nature of the Pastoral Conversation

This question of the specific nature of the pastoral conversation has received a great deal of attention in Europe, especially since the end of World War II. Taken together, this has contributed to a deepening and enlarging of our understanding of this problem.

Within the Netherlands first place must be given to the inaugural address of E. L. Smelik, "The Conversation in Pastoral Theology." [1] First of all, Smelik speaks about *conversation in a general sense* as "the most direct spiritual contact between people," pointing out that conversation, the really deep conversation, is withering and shriveling away in our present-day world. Next he deals with the *philosophical conversation* as Socrates and Kierkegaard knew it, in which the philosophical dialogue as they practiced it

[1] "Het Gesprek in de Pastorale Theologie," Nijkerk, 1949.

"kept human thinking in a flowing movement." The *revelational dialogue* is then described, in which man in the first place is the one spoken to by God. This dialogue between God and man "cannot be considered a conversation of two equal partners. God's speaking rises high above the speaking of man." In the following briefly discussed *mystical conversation* "some form of a visionary experienced encounter is often found, in which the soul holds a dialogue." Next Smelik turns to *pastoral conversation* about which he first of all says that its starting point is to be found in the fact that "in the nearness of Christ the communication between men is brought to a more radical openness than ever took place elsewhere." The relationship from person to person in all its aspects changes essentially. Smelik devotes some excellent pages to this subject.

When Smelik tries to define the specific nature of the pastoral conversation and also to differentiate it from other forms of conversation, he finds that "the pastor is a person with a charge." He does not carry on the conversation *"auctoritate sua* (not on his own authority), but in the name of his Master who sent him. . . . The pastoral conversation is one of the forms, no more and no less, in which Christ continues his dialogue with the world until the end of time." Smelik wants to distinguish the pastoral conversation from genuine psychological conversation. The latter takes place within the boundaries of the intrapsychic, and it is concerned with the self-deliverance of the troubled person. Smelik is of the opinion, however, that when matters are gone into deeply enough, even the psychologist and the psychiatrist come to a point where the *patient* no longer needs any treatment, but where he needs guidance. "Then the question is not only whether biological vitality can win, or whether social adaptation is realized in a satisfactory manner, but whether a truly delivering word and meaningful charge can be proclaimed." This leads us again to the background and the most essential aspect of the pastoral conversation: "The proclamation of the Word that is not ours, but God's, the Word of forgiveness, renewal, and hope, that was and is spoken in Christ."

J. H. van den Berg has also discussed this subject most helpfully in his article: "Conversation and the Specific Nature of Pastoral Conversation." [2] The greater part of the article (the conversation) is also to be found in the collection, *The Person and the World*.[3] One of the conditions of the conversation according to van den Berg is the asymmetry of the speakers. "If there is a typical asymmetry of partners, then the conversation has a typical character." For example, take the relationship between lovers, between teacher and pupil, doctor and patient. "The form of conversation in these and so many other contacts is completely determined by the form typical of the asymmetry of both speakers." It has been said that the specific nature of pastoral conversation was completely determined by the asymmetry of the partners—the pastor in conversation with the "layman," the parishioner. Then, according to van den Berg, it is the human point of contact to which the pastor appeals, for instance, the pastor responds to the need for consolation, the necessity of admonition, etc. The conversation is then completely determined by the asymmetry of the human communication.

But, van den Berg continues, the primary psychological objection is that experience has convinced us that the pastoral conversation differs completely from all other forms of conversation. Here he cites E. L. Smelik:

This communication is not to be considered as friendship, nor as enmity, nor as sympathy, nor as indifference. In this relation the pastor must be

[2] "Het Gesprek en de bijzondere Aard van het Pastorale Gesprek," *Theologie en Practijk*, 1950, Nos. 9 and 10.

[3] *Persoon en Wereld* (Utrecht, 1953).

able to be more loving than a friend, sometimes harder than an enemy, more comforting than a mother, more stern than a father, more understanding than a pedagogue, more indifferent than someone who passes by.

The relationship between the minister and his parishioners "is therefore not determined by psychology." [4] Further van den Berg argues that the pastoral conversation is not of this world, it is a nonpsychological conversation even though it does not lack the influence of certain psychological data.

It is a conversation, that may trample on psychology, that at times reveals a remarkable infidelity to all psychological experience. . . . The pastoral conversation is a strange conversation. It is constituted, not by the being together that realizes itself as a world, but by the Strange Word, by this Third Party who is present when two are together in his name.

But at the same time this strange conversation forms our home preeminently. It creates a new scope in which all human things appear in a new light, the scope of the church. "The pastoral conversation is a conversation within the church." For it is constituted by the Strange Word. This Strange Word itself, however, does not form the direct subject of the conversation.[5] The conversation is about the daily affairs which occupy the person's mind, but the special feature is that these affairs are confronted here with the Strange Word. However, an outsider need not notice the strangeness of the pastoral conversation. Rather the danger threatens from the other side—especially by choosing the Strange Word as the direct subject of the conversation, the pastor can make it a thor-

---

[4] *De Wegen der Kerk. De Brieven aan Timotheus, Titus en Filemon* (*The Ways of the Church. The Letters to Timothy, Titus, and Philemon*) (Nijkerk, 1940), p. 64.

[5] Later on van den Berg expressed himself differently. I have in mind his essay "Pastoral Care and Psychotherapy" (*The Student World*, No. 1, 1954), where we find the words: "He (the pastor) talks till he thinks the time is ripe to pronounce explicitly the Word which during the whole conversation was tacitly implied." p. 84.

oughly "wordly" (that is to say in this connection "sinful") conversation. "The *disputare de deo,* for instance, has nothing to do with pastoral conversation." To these reflections by van den Berg may be added a reference to his Preface in my book, *Chapters from Pastoral Psychology.*[6] There he summarizes the difference between pastoral and psychotherapeutic conversation as follows:

Psychologists and psychotherapists work in charge of the client (or in charge of the human agency which is responsible for the client or the patient), but not the pastor; he works in charge of another one, of the other whose name is written with a capital. When the psychologist speaks with the client, there are two; when the pastor speaks, there are three. That is the difference.

To this discussion may be added a few words about the views of H. R. Wijngaarden, professor of psychology at the Free University in Amsterdam. I do not quote from any publication but from discussions with him personally and within the Commission of Pastoral Care. The difference between the conversational situation with a pastor and a psychologist is, according to Wijngaarden, determined by the following:

The psychologist renders his services to a client, *a.* at the request of the client, *b.* on the basis of his expert knowledge, *c.* with the aim to help the client find an answer to the questions and problems which confront him.

The pastor renders his services to a parishioner, *a.* whether or not at the parishioner's request—for it can be his duty to seek contact with someone unrequested, *b.* not on the basis of his expert knowledge, but on the basis of his being commissioned by the

---

[6] *Hoofdstukken uit de Pastorale Psychologie* (Utrecht, 1959). From now on I will refer to this book as *Pastoral Psychology.*

church, c. with the purpose of standing by the parishioner as a representative of his church, and in place of Christ, standing by the parishioner in his joy, sorrow, and problems of life, in order to manifest that under all circumstances Christ is present. The condition for such standing by is the understanding of the other person.

Whereas it is the aim of the psychologist to help the other person become more independent, for the pastor it is important to help the other find the right relationship with God and his fellowmen.

Outside the Netherlands in western Europe, our attention is especially drawn to two books. The first is the book of Eduard Thurneysen, *Die Lehre von der Seelsorge*.[7] The book of Thurneysen should be considered as the most important application of the Barthian theological position to pastoral care. It certainly introduced a new period in Europe, not only giving the pastoral conversation a central place but also trying to give room to the psychological aspects of it. This has been the value of this publication for the European development in this field. On the other hand, it is too dogmatic in its approach and does not take the empirical situation enough into account. Therefore, it offers too little help to the person who finds himself confronted with the specific task: I have to carry on pastoral conversations, but how do I learn to do it? Another important German publication may be mentioned here: Adelheid Rensch, *Das seelsorgerliche Gespräch*.[8] Adelheid Rensch is a psychologist. She is a lecturer on pastoral psychology at the University of Leipzig. In her publication we find a penetrating theological study of the pastoral conversation, in which we notice that as far as the psychology is concerned, only the European psy-

[7] (Zürich: Evangelischer Verlag A. G. Zollikon, 1946). The translation was published in the United States as *A Theology of Pastoral Care* (Richmond: John Knox Press, 1961).

[8] (Göttingen: Vandenhoeck & Ruprecht, 1963).

chological tradition is found, while American publications and influence in this field have been neglected. The book gives important theoretical reflections but little practical help and no mention is made of the indispensable clinical training. From both these books we can learn how much we need one another in the field of pastoral care and that American and European cooperation and exchange should prove very fruitful.

Two books on this subject were published in the French language by Roman Catholic authors during the past few years: Raymond Hostie, S. J., *L'Entretien Pastoral* (*Pastoral Conversations*) and A. Godin, S.J., *La Relation Humaine dans Le Dialogue Pastoral* (*Human Relationship in the Pastoral Conversation*).[9] American influence is evident in both books and the importance of clinical training is clearly put, but so far they have had little practical consequences in the French-speaking countries.

The Specific Nature
of the Pastoral Conversation

Before trying to formulate the specific nature of the pastoral conversation, it might be helpful to dwell for a moment upon the adjective "pastoral," especially the combination "pastoral conversation." In the first place, it is possible to mean by the qualification "pastoral," everything that a pastor does in his function as pastor. The pastor who calls at the homes of his parishioners has a pastoral conversation, simply because this conversation is based on the *pastoral* charge which he received from his church.

However, it is also possible that with the definition "pastoral" a special qualification of the conversation itself is given, that is, about the significance it had for the person concerned. For him that

[9] Both books were published by Desclée de Brouwer, 1963.

conversation was a guiding to, a testimony of the Great Pastor (Shepherd) Jesus Christ. In this conversation something was noticeable of the safety which Christ offers and the way which he shows us. Perhaps the person who held the conversation had no pastoral charge, and therefore it was not a pastoral conversation in the formal sense. It is self-evident that a conversation can be a pastoral conversation as described in the first meaning (for instance, a conversation between pastor and parishioner) without it being as described in the second meaning, and vice versa.

With this distinction in mind, it is possible to get nearer to the specific nature of the pastoral conversation in the following summary:

1. The pastoral conversation takes place, because the church—and through the church, Christ—commissioned the pastor. This awareness of not speaking on your own authority but in service of the Lord appears to me to be *the* fundamental presupposition.

2. The pastoral conversation finds its fulfillment there where the Strange Word is heard, where the Third Party enters the conversation, where people know themselves to be standing in God's presence. This, in fact, can mean that even when the first condition (the commission of the church) is not formally satisfied, the second condition still can be met in a conversation with, for instance, a physician, a psychologist, a social worker, etc.

3. The pastoral conversation may cover a very wide range of topics. Of course, we may say that where the central questions of religion and life, the all-important questions, are discussed, we are also more existentially involved in the real pastoral conversation than when on the occasion of a call the advantages of a Chevrolet over a Ford are discussed because the parishioner is planning to buy a car. But we should not be mistaken. The question of *whether* the

parishioner (or the pastor) will buy a car *can* be a much more meaningful topic for a pastoral conversation than a conversation about predestination or about atonement. The topic itself is to a certain extent irrelevant. That which matters is what the question means in the life of this person, whether and how it *touches his heart and soul.* This means that many questions of a completely "wordly" character can lead to a deeply moving pastoral conversation. Quite a few "religious questions" and theological subjects may be discussed in the pastoral conversation. However, in actuality these often are discussed only superficially and do not lead to a deeply moving pastoral conversation. How often do not the pastoral workers walk into that trap! So what is peculiar to the pastoral conversation is that all problems, even the ordinary things of everyday life, are always confronted with the gospel and are put in the light of faith. We can also formulate it this way: Whatever may come up and in however a natural, level-headed and reasonable way the things are discussed, ultimately the salvation of men is that which matters. *Even in everyday life* it concerns *the ultimate reality,* however obscure it may be.

By this time it should have become apparent that the difference between the conversations of the pastor and those of the other professions whose aim it is to be of help to people cannot be found, and surely not completely, in the *subjects* of the conversation. Neither may the difference be found in the idea, that only in the conversation with the pastor God would be present, and not elsewhere. How then should we define it? Here are some considerations besides those which already have been mentioned.

1. The pastor compared with the psychotherapist: Here the therapist's expert knowledge is of importance. Generally, people only turn to him with serious problems in which psychic complica-

tions and conflicts are clearly evident. Furthermore, the time involved is also important. The pastor who is responsible for his parish, generally cannot start counseling which will take months or years (even though he would be qualified for this through study and training), not even if the motive would be to help the other person live with God.

2. As far as the differentiation between pastor and social worker is concerned, sometimes this will be evident, other times it will be difficult to define it in practice. Now I am thinking in particular of social work through the church as it is known in Holland. The expert knowledge in regard to all social aspects of problems is, amongst others, an important factor. Here there are dangers threatening from the different sides—from the side of ministers, members of the church board and parishioners who do not recognize the special meaning of the social work of the church and who ignore the social worker of the church in practice or use him for odd jobs; from the side of the social worker, who sometimes does not see the function of the pastor and, for instance, contends that marriage and family problems belong to the social worker, religious problems belong to the pastor. By doing and by being prepared to cooperate and to learn from one another, we have to find our way. For many a social worker in the service of the church it sometimes seems to be a difficult matter to discover how his specific background (it is the *church*, it is *Christ*, who is the commissioner) is one of the factors which determines his conversation, to which extent and in which manner the pastoral aspect can come to its full advantage in his conversations. It seems to me that many things are not clear, and training and supervision do not give the social worker enough insight into these questions. Attention to a psychological training in counseling and at the same time doing justice to the evangelical charge have to come to full advantage in the

education and supervision of the social worker as much as in that of the pastor, even though the situation for the two groups is different.

3. As far as the differentiation between the pastor and the physician (including the psychiatrist as a medical specialist) is concerned, the specific nature of the physician's profession is the concentration on the recovery of the patient. Also the conversations he has—possibly his psychotherapy—are concentrated on that. As a physician his ultimate goal is not to guide a person to God and help him live accordingly. Of course, the Christian physician is aware that salvation is more important than recovery, and he will hope that the recovery may serve the salvation, the integration in its deepest sense. He shall, as a Christian, where this is justified, be able to speak an explicit pastoral word, a word of forgiveness, a word of consolation, a word of encouragement. But he is not an incompetent *physician*, if he does not do so. I certainly reject the opinion, as presented by some authors, that only a physician who *believes* is able to do his work well—a tendency which is found for instance in the book of the German psychiatrist Hans Gödan, *Christ and Hippocrates*.[10]

So, quite often pastor and physician will discuss the same difficulties and questions. Their aims are different; the one is concentrated on recovery and the other on salvation, while at the same time they know that this *differentiation* does not mean a *separation*. The pastor *can* by pastoral (possibly pastoral-therapeutic) conversations also serve the physical and spiritual health of the other; the physician *can* by his (possibly medical-therapeutic) conversations indirectly serve the salvation of the other, because, owing to the inner growth toward freedom, he is (psychologically speaking) better able to make an authentic religious choice.

[10] *Christus und Hippokrates* (Stuttgart, 1958).

Should the Pastor Be Different from Others?

It is self-evident that the question of the specific nature of the pastoral conversation is not a matter of only "theoretical reflections" for the pastor, but that it concerns here the question of how he performs an important part of his daily work. If I am right, it is often a problem for many pastors to gain insight into the relationship of their personality on the one side and the specific nature of their office on the other side. Nowadays, there is often a tendency to tell the pastors and ministers that they should behave as "ordinary" people. This is an evident reaction to a situation in which the ministers of the church distinguished themselves in an obvious manner from the parishioner—in dress, behavior, style, etc. As a reaction, a more normal behavior is expected, sometimes with the result, however, that some exaggerate acting as "ordinary" persons, and can be easily recognized as pastors by their forced manners. This sometimes expresses itself by showy modern dress, and a somewhat jovial behavior.

In this situation we also often meet ministers who say: "They may say what they like. They have told us endlessly that by all means we have to behave as others do, but they forget that often the problem for us is that we have so much difficulty with the 'wondrous office' as it is sometimes called—a strange office. How do we express that in our life, in our daily contacts, in our conversations as pastors with others?" The reader will notice that here again the question of what is peculiar to the pastoral conversation immediately comes up. What is this difference, this specific nature of the pastoral conversation? What is involved here is the misunderstanding which assumes that the different nature of the message should be translated into different behavior on the part of the minister, possibly even into a different way of speaking. But isn't it a relief for the pastor to know that all that is expected of him is the same as is expected of everybody else, that he must do his work well? A doctor has to examine the patient conscientiously, make a diagnosis, etc. A pastor has conscientiously to prepare a service, the lessons for confirmation classes, have an attentive ear for the problems of others. In this he has to serve devotedly the agency he represents, as every other representative has to do.

This is not to minimize the meaning which the message holds for the pastor himself, but this must not interfere too much with his work. I mean that if the pastor was wrong in his personal life on Saturday or had to struggle with a personal doubt, then he should not think, "Now I can't possibly preach tomorrow! I won't be able to hold the pastoral conversation with Mr. X. tonight." No, the work goes on, and he has to do it, regardless of the ups and downs in his personal life. Naturally, there is a limit. At a given moment there may be not only ups and downs, but the pastor may permanently decide that he does not believe in his ministry any more and choose another course, fully aware of what he does. Then he has to accept the consequences. But as long as the ultimate limit has not been reached, he has to continue faithfully, regardless of his own uncertainty and unbelief. Examples of these problems of the pastor can also be found in modern literature—for instance, in the works of Graham Greene and Kaj Munk (the Danish pastor, author, and martyr). Of the latter we especially recall his play *Love* in which the unbelieving pastor Kargo (who is in love with the wife of the burgomaster) in a conversation with the bishop and the dean frankly professes his unbelief and to the startled question of the dean, "But why in heaven's name then are you a minister?" he answers, "To help the people by trying to make them believe that God exists." He preaches the gospel wholeheartedly, regardless of his unbelief. "Because, when I was at a sickbed, when I stood in the pulpit, and saw these faces, which I knew so well and knew why those wrinkles were carved in them, then my urge to help and my fear to disappoint them was so great that I could do it."

The Symbolic Meaning of the Pastor

When speaking of the specific nature of the pastoral conversation we must also pay attention to the symbolic meaning of the pastor. Who turns to the pastor does something different from the person who turns to the social worker, psychologist, or physician. The pastor stands for, symbolizes, represents, the Christian community, Christ, God. Of course, the person whom he meets may not have realized this consciously—perhaps there are only vague feelings and associations. But these can be very important for the conversation. The symbolic meaning which the pastor has for a person can bring with it many difficulties and possibilities. Many earlier experiences with the church, all sorts of religious notions, ideas, fears, expectations with regard to God, are involved when he turns to the pastor. We may say that on the one hand the parishioner comes with already existing and clear-cut expectations; on the other hand we bring them to life, correct them or extinguish them by the manner in which we are indeed "a reference" for the other person to God. An additional complication may be that the manner in which the pastor bears witness to God by his words, belies his actual personal attitude. A pastor may, for instance, emphatically speak of God's forgiveness and patience, while the parishioner feels that the pastor himself is actually nonaccepting, moralizing, authoritative, impatient. In such a case the decisive factor will be not the formulated message, but the message as it is evident in the pastor's contact with others, in the way he incarnates it.

181

Must the Pastor Himself
Believe in His Work?

Elsewhere in this book the reader will find a discussion of the conditions which must be met, if the pastor is to be able to carry on a pastoral conversation. I will mention one condition which I think is appropriate to discuss now. The pastor himself must have *faith* in the pastoral conversation, in the possibilities which it has, and, of course, he should do this in a realistic manner. Now the same is true, naturally, for all people who professionally carry on conversations. I should like to remark that, in my opinion, many conversations lead to little or nothing because the persons who hold them (social worker, psychologist, physician, etc.) have no faith in the client and in the conversation with him. In the field which has my greatest personal interest, besides the ministry, and that which I can judge best, the field of psychotherapy, this surely counts. That therapy sometimes has little result is, amongst other reasons, caused by the attitude of the psychotherapist toward the client. Through the years I have seen some startling examples of this. It is also a common observation that whether or not the psychotherapist belongs to a Christian church is not at all the deciding factor. I point this out because I often notice that ministers, when referring someone to a psychotherapist, make sure it is one who belongs to a church. I am inclined to recognize the significance of someone's belief, not only for his psychotherapeutic work, but as well for the sake of a common spiritual background of patient (client) and the therapist. But I should like to add immediately—there are psychiatrists and psychologists who belong to a church and who profess the Christian religion, but about whom it definitely could not be said that they regard their patients with faith, respect, and patience. And there are non-Christians amongst the psychotherapists whose whole attitude in their psychotherapeutic work shows more of the spirit of the gospel than some of their "Christian" colleagues.

In this connection it is worth mentioning a lecture given by A. Maeder at the International Psychotherapeutic Congress in Leyden on "The Role of the Affective Contact in Psychotherapy." Maeder points out that there are psychotherapists who during the course of years have become very skeptical about the possibilities of psychotherapy and the changes which can be expected of it for the client or patient. They regard the patient quite rapidly as unsuitable for psychotherapy, as a person with whom it is difficult to get contact. In short, as a rather "hopeless case." According to Maeder, they act as if this unsuitability, this difficulty in the contact, is an objectively given characteristic of the patient, without realizing that in establishing the contact two persons are involved. The character, the attitude of that moment, the mood of the psychotherapist, are all very important and have to be taken into account, as much as the situation of the person seeking help. Maeder further argues that there are psychotherapists who became skeptical of the effectiveness of the psychotherapy and who base their opinion on all sorts of apparently strictly medical considerations and conclusions. But when the matter is considered more closely, it is often noticed that they are influenced by their own personal problems which they do not recognize themselves, but which influence the contact with the patient and even their diagnosis. And as a consequence of the worsening of the results, they no longer believe in their work, in the possibilities of psychotherapy so that the basic condition for a successful therapy is no longer present.

All this can be transposed to the pastoral relation. For the pastoral conversation an attitude of love, acceptance, patience, faith, and respect is required. It is necessary to have faith in the possibilities of the pastoral conversation. The specific character of the pastoral conversation means that we hope to stand with the other person in God's light. That means that this conversation takes place in a sphere of faith and prayer. Even if these are still unattainable and impossible realities for the other, for the pastor it is different. He prays for this other person. He has faith in the other because behind the life of this person he sees God, who does not forsake the work that his hand began for this man. That is why he believes that this pastoral conversation makes sense. He believes that a person can change, through pastoral conversation. If he can no longer believe in that, possibly because he thinks he never notices anything of it, then this very attitude becomes a reason for self-examination and for seriously putting the question to himself: Is it possibly my fault—my lack of faith, my lack of hope, my poverty of love—that the pastoral conversation I have with the other is marked by spiritual impotence? For one of the essential characteristics of the pastoral conversation is to be found in this, that it is a *hopeful* conversation!

IX

Distinctive Resources in
Pastoral Conversation

The pastor does not stand in an isolated position with the other person during the pastoral conversation. The "neutral" psychotherapist does to a certain extent. The psychotherapeutic conversation takes place within the safe enclosure of the four walls. In all likelihood therapist and client did not know each other beforehand. In this relationship which develops, a lot may happen that may become important in the life of the client. But after the last session he closes the door behind him and with that the matter has ended, except for the last bill he will receive.

The pastor finds himself in a quite different situation. He receives the person because he has been commissioned by his church. He also does this as representative of the church. He is not only concerned with the person's psychic conflicts and problems but with his faith, so that the other will learn to see his own life in God's light, discover the church of Christ, and learn to recognize his fellow man as his brother. This means that the pastor in the pastoral conversation must have knowledge of specific pastoral resources, which may be of importance to the other person.

The Community of the Church

From the beginning Jesus Christ gathered a community around himself; this was the church, the Body of the Lord. God has no children living by themselves, who have nothing to do with their fellow men. The Christians know a new communion with God and with one another (compare the Great Commandment of Christ, the Acts of the Apostles, the apostolic letters, etc.). Pastorate, apostolate and diaconate also arise from this communion. They presuppose this being with the other. These are not only basic sociological factors. They are the fundamental laws of the kingdom of God.

This communion of the church is very important for each of its members. The numerous complaints and reproaches addressed to the church by the people, that they were left out in the cold and were offered no fellowship when life became too difficult for them alone, show us that people feel by intuition something of the significance of the church as a community. And with this we are in the midst of the problems of modern life. For today community has not only become a problem for the community of the church, but in all other aspects as well. Society abandons the individual, no longer binds him, no longer binds individuals together. People no longer feel themselves to be accepted as full members of a community, either inside or outside of the church. This gives many people a feeling of great inner discord, if not of inner disunion. It makes them maladjusted, uncertain, aggressive, neurotic. These problems do not stop at the doors of the church.

The community of the church is often not very convincing, either to the parishioner or to the outsider. And within the church an additional number of aggravating factors are added to this. The continuing disunity of Christianity destroys the conviction behind all the beautiful-sounding words about truth, community, love and unity. But on the other hand the Christian church is and shall remain a Christian *community* in numerous manifestations, a spiritual and therefore an actual reality of the first order for countless people. And also the many pastoral conversations which are held daily all over the world are held because the Christian church is in this world. It is evident that the pastoral conversation, even if it is a strictly personal conversation, has as a presupposition and background the community of the church and the hope that it will lead the other (back) to this community. By this we do not mean that we have only to take people up in normal parish life. It is alarming how easily many people, as a matter of course, assume that the structure of community life as it stands is such that it is possible for everyone to find his or her place. Personally, I am of the opinion that the structure of parish life in the Netherlands nowadays is in many respects still a structure of the past. Because of this many Christians of today do not feel at home in it. Instead of always branding this as disloyalty toward the church of Christ (this *may* be so!), we may also find that people reject the forms and rules of the church of yesterday (which one finds time and time again in the church of today) but possibly are quite prepared to work for the church of tomorrow.

I should like to point out, on the basis of many experiences in pastoral conversation, the necessity for a more differentiated building up of parish life and its working methods. I often experienced it as an urgent need, when having one or more pastoral conversations with people from other parishes, that they would very

187

much like to find their place in the parish, without there being a reasonable possibility for it in their environment. The argument that a person simply has to adapt himself to the church in his or her place of residence must be rejected. If we consider more closely what people who say this mean by "church," then it appears to be a very distinct group of Christians, doubtlessly also part of the church, but who with an uncanny certainty take it for granted that their own dogmatic definiteness, their own traditional forms, are the most suitable "spiritual home" for everyone. I am afraid that church life of nowadays is all too often adjusted to "the average churchgoer," and therefore so many fellow Christians leave the church.

If we want to lead people from the pastoral conversation back to the community of the congregation, then I consider the following points as absolutely necessary:[1]

1. The church and parish life should have great multiformity. In our multiformed, complex community life only a parish which takes that into account can be the spiritual home of people.

2. The community of the church should be more than only a liturgical community in order to be a really spiritual home for the individual. It is necessary that between the individual and the small community of marriage and family, and the congregation in its official worship, there be small communities whose responsibility it is to take care that people do not isolate themselves in their own egocentric existence, and furthermore do not limit themselves only to participation in the conventionalized liturgical community. Those small communities should entertain no more than twelve to fifteen members, and they should be "open" communities in

---

[1] For the following considerations I am greatly indebted to Prof. Hoekendijk. In view of the fact that these thoughts come from remarks made at conferences and private conversations, I cannot state exactly where I cite him or where I give my own viewpoints.

the sense of being directed outward toward other people, not merely verbally, but first of all by what they *are*. These communities also have to be ecumenical so that members of different churches may belong to them. It is evident that in this situation the pastor no longer is the man who has to do everything. On the contrary, what is most important here is the responsibility of the parish members themselves. They are one another's shepherds, servants, and apostles. When he reflects on the pastoral conversation, it is of great importance that the pastor shall not see it as his duty to, within the limits of the conversation, give another person all the help he needs. This would be much too heavy a task. Considered from the psychological standpoint it would be unhealthy and impossible, a much too heavy psychic burden. But also from a theological standpoint it is a misconception. In the first place, a person is helped, supported, accompanied, and comforted by and through the community of brothers and sisters. But sometimes it is necessary to have a conversation in private, and sometimes it is well that this is done by the pastor. It is important, and it even may be a necessity that this possibility exists. But then we return as soon as possible to the community of the church. This community is too seldom realized. And for this reason pastors can, in the pastoral conversation, sometimes be of very little help. This community which now would have to be a curative and helping medium for pastoral help, often functions very badly. We could say: The better the community of the church functions, the lesser will be the need for a personal pastoral conversation.

Liturgy

We just pointed out that the community of the parish should be more than a liturgical community which gathers on Sundays.

It is now important to stress that the liturgical community is of great importance, from the viewpoint of the pastoral conversation. All the functions of the church originate in the heart of the liturgy, the Holy Communion where everything that Christ has to say to us, has done for us, and will be for us, is recapitulated and given in a few words and acts. It is the hope of the pastor, in his consulting room, to help his fellow man find his way to the place where the community gathers for worship. Someone who participates as a believer in the liturgy, the prayer, the adoration, the Holy Communion, may be strengthened beyond words by it, and it may also help him find his own way in life. This last sentence will not be understood by many—even by members of the church. For others it will contain a truth with which they will agree wholeheartedly. I should like to quote the following words from Romano Guardini which, in the first place, concern man in his adoration of God, but which can be extended to include man in his participation in the liturgy in all its aspects:

The guarantee for the purity of the spirit is the adoration of God. As long as man worships God, as long as he bows before God as for The One who "is worthy to receive the glory and the honor and the power," because He is the True and Holy One, until then he will be kept from deceit. Purity and health of spirit are very strong but also—such is man— very vulnerable and easily tempted. He needs protection. There must be something, through which good and evil, pure and impure become distinct and clear to the human spirit time and time again. The fact that man does not do the good that he has recognized as such is bad and makes him "guilty for the Judgment." But the confusion in relation to truth itself is incomparably worse; the deceit is in the eyes because it is in the spirit itself. Therefore, there must be something through which the heart can renew itself again and again in the truth, the spirit can cleanse itself, the eyes can be purified, the character can bind itself.

That is the adoration. For man nothing is more important than that he learns to bow before God in his inner self, to make room for Him, so that He can raise Himself and can be the True One, because He is worthy of it. To think, to confirm with the inner self that God is worthy of the adoration, seen from His truth, endlessly, unconditionally —this is holy and great and restores to health, entirely.[2]

That the practical difficulties are many, even here, we know. There are countless people who will not find their spiritual home in the average church service—in the previously mentioned limited meaning. Here a legitimate differentiation is necessary. For the rest, in order not to repeat myself, I refer to the remarks on this subject in my book *Pastoral Psychology*. It seems to be a fact, however, that just those persons who in our time rediscover and practice the "small community" at the same time also return to the liturgical community, in prayer services, communion services, etc. I think that we see many examples of it. It is as if many rediscover the connection between that which much too often and much too long has been separated. Furthermore, it is evident that the transition of the liturgical community to these small forms of community is fluid. Especially noticeable is how nowadays these small communities are often called "home communities," and know all kinds of liturgical acts (prayer, Bible readings and discussion, song) while the possibility of Holy Communion is being considered by many.

Prayer

In many cases the pastor will speak about prayer with people coming to him in different situations. It is striking that numerous

[2] *Der Herr* (*The Lord*), (Utrecht: Het Spectrum, 1960), pp. 632 ff.

people of today have unlearned something at the cost of their true self, which always belonged to the essential possibilities of the human soul—and still does, even though many do not see it—prayer.

We can talk about prayer in two different ways. In the first place, for a Christian, life itself is prayer, is willingness to be open for the God, whose voice is calling, is dialogue with the reality of God. But this way of life concentrates and condenses at certain moments to the act of prayer in a narrower sense. For a moment we retire from the throbbing rush of life, the avalanche of events, the often chaotic and restless diversity of daily affairs, and we put ourselves in concentration before God. We fold our hands, hands which can murder, steal, mutilate, but also comfort, and caress; we fold them together so that they will not do anything anymore (Or are they now doing the deepest and most ineffable thing that human hands can do?). Mostly we close our eyes—those eyes which can look eagerly, greedily, without respect upon the other and the world, but also quietly, respectfully and seeking communication; we close them so that they will see nothing (Or do they now see all?). We kneel devoutly or we stand before God or we sit relaxed and waiting, and we have a dialogue, we speak, and we are listening. That we speak may be noticed, that we listen is for many a problem, if not ridiculous. The presupposition of this is that there can be a silence which is filled with the presence and word of God. This already involves a faithful attitude as a response to a word which was spoken to us: "Adam, where are you, who are you, what do you do with the life that was given to you? Do you know that you are responsible for it, that your life has to be a response to my call?" But to go into this further would be going beyond the context of this book.

What is the *psychological* significance of prayer? Men seek in this the peace, the relaxation (which as a phase may involve great anxiety and struggle), in which he can concentrate upon a new communion with his fellow man, the world, himself, and—above and in all this—with God. For the person who has learned to pray, prayer is a great and inexhaustible source of strength which can make his life a prayer, a dialogue with reality. There are numerous people who have learned in difficult situations that prayer has an irreplaceable significance in the daily struggle of life. Because of that the meaning of prayer can be so significant. On the other hand, it is often found that prayer is a rather barren and discouraging matter for many, rather a monologue than a dialogue. All this is often caused by an immature and infantile religious life. In short, we may say: Prayer can be a source of strength, life, and renewal; but on the other hand, the immature and egocentric prayer, which in the deepest sense is "unbelieving," will harm the person spiritually and psychically, yes, in his totality.

W. J. Berger has discussed the problems of prayer in an illuminating way by comparing them with the problems faced in growing up.[3] Every time a person stands on the threshold of a new experience, which opens the possibility of growth, he must overcome resistance against parting from the old, and against the new risk and the new development, which we want but which at the same time frightens us. Similar risks are involved, Berger declares, in the experience of prayer, and they are often raised by persons during pastoral conversations on prayer.

1. In the first place, there are people who pray only when in difficulties. For the rest prayer is of little or no importance in their lives. But are they not like children, who only ask when some unpleasant thing has to be removed? Don't they then live in the childishly primitive pleasure-pain scheme?

---

[3] *Contactblad van de Aalmoezeniers bij de Inrichtingen van Justitie,* Vol. 10, No. 6.

2. Another problem is: God does not answer my prayer, even though I pray for things of importance. But is this not the attitude: God must do what I want him to do? Do "I" not stand in the center in a wrong way? When I consider that my requests are reasonable and yet they are not answered, then I could ask myself whether *I* am being unreasonable, unreasonable to such an extent that I prevent my Father from giving that which I ask for. I ask reasonable things, but can it be that I don't get them because I make myself inaccessible for them?

With a few examples I should like to illustrate these prayer difficulties. A person addicted to liquor says in a pastoral conversation that he always prays God to keep him from drinking, and he also asks the pastor to pray with him for it. At the same time he is not prepared to follow the advice of the physician and the pastor to submit himself to a cure. A woman with homosexual problems speaks about her praying for it, "God does not answer." At the same time she refuses to accept psychotherapy, even though it would seem desirable. A married couple having marital problems, have been praying about it for years. But even though the strong neurotic components are brought to their attention, they refuse to seek help. All these cases concern matters which are very important for these people, but their own unreasonableness is that they are not prepared to do that which reasonably lies within the realm of human possibilities and therefore should be done.

3. A third problem with prayer: My prayer is worthless because my heart is not in it. When I hear other people talk about it, I understand that it means a great deal to them, but when I pray myself my heart is barren and arid. The questions which Berger then raises, boil down to this: Is my heart ever with something or somebody? Is my heart ever really open? Or do I keep myself from letting my emotions speak—knowingly or unknowingly? Are there

childish, unreasonable anxieties which keep me from understanding and sympathizing with everything which reveals the meaning of life and the purpose of God to me?

4. The fourth difficulty which Berger discusses is of the person who says, "I do not pray, because there is no God. And if he does exist, he is a power with whom I am at odds, because things in life are no different than they are." Is the heart of the matter not the question: What does matter? Me? That I want to be the norm and standard of everything? Or am I prepared to learn to surrender myself, questioning, listening, believing? "The whole human walk of life," says Berger in this connection, "is a proceeding from childish self-centeredness to serving and being available. Alas, it is tragic that many pastors believe they are protecting faith most effectively by keeping people childish in matters of faith and conscience, so that they keep them from reaching adulthood and block their relationship with God."

If people with difficulties like these come to us, then often we shall not be able to help them in one session. The point is that the person has to recognize his immaturity. For that he will have to learn to understand his walk of life. The inner growth has to get started again. Steps ahead have to be taken, decisions have to be made. Think of the prayer of Jesus, "Not my will, but thine, be done." While praying he made a decision, but in the same way it is true to say that because of this decision he could pray. I believe that every difficulty with prayer only then finds its solution when the decision with which I am confronted is made, when the next step is taken. Sometimes we have to grow toward the next step, and it is the task of the pastor to create the right climate for it.

In my opinion, the above pastoral psychological considerations are quite important, so that it seemed advisable to quote them extensively, with some personal remarks in between. Here it is also stressed that the pastoral conversation demands great *pastoral wisdom* as well as a *psychologically differentiated conversation*— even if only to discover with the other person the *place and significance* this problem takes *in his life.*

Two other remarks may close off the discussion on prayer in connection with the pastoral conversation. As pastor one must realize to what degree prayer is often a "charged" subject for many persons, because of influences during youth. They *had* to pray, maybe in a manner which they did not appreciate nor accept inwardly at all. Especially in certain Roman Catholic and orthodox Protestant circles this may play an important part. All sorts of negative feelings are associated with the theme "prayer." First of all, there will have to be a "disassociating" before a truly "to the point" conversation is possible, let alone that a person can do something with prayer. This ties in with the above remark; the *place and significance of the problem in this person's life* has to be brought out into the open, and for that, a therapeutic—and that is in line with the thought of this book—counseling phase can be of great importance.

What is the place of prayer in the pastoral conversation? Often a difficult question! There are conversations which as a matter of course and with inner certainty lead to prayer. There are others where this is not the case, and then it should not be done. First, of all, prayer should not be forced as a part of the pastoral conversation. Neither should it be artificially avoided. Prayer *can* be of great importance within the pastoral conversation. It also may be experienced as superfluous; it even may annoy the other person. Again, listening will have to show the way.

What should we do if the other person asks that we pray with him (possibly mentioning the subject of prayer), while the pastor has the feeling that this is not the right moment? I believe he should refuse quietly and explain this refusal tactfully and with love. An example of such a situation might arise in connection with a marriage of which it is evident that divorce may be considered the lesser of two evils. The husband (a very anxious, compulsive, neurotic man, who has a love affair with another woman and mistreats his wife), asks the pastor in a conversation whether the pastor will pray with him that his wife will not take this sinful decision lest the punishment of God will fall upon them. The pastor cannot comply with this request. Neither may he comply by praying with the man about something different than was asked for (for instance, praying that the man may gain better insight). That is an abuse of prayer. So, generally, it cannot be said that every request to pray together should be complied with. Here again what must be considered is *the place and significance of this problem in the person's life.*

Confession and Absolution

This subject, too, requires that we be concerned with some pastoral psychological considerations.

1. In the first place it is well to differentiate between catharsis only (abreaction) and confession, by which we mean particularly private, personal, or auricular confession. Confessing always presupposes the confession of one's sins before God in the presence of another person, who acts by virtue of his office, in other words, listens and speaks in the name of God. This is the case even when one parishioner listens to the confession of his fellow parishioner by reason of the general priesthood of all believers. To listen to the confession of another, to speak the word of forgiveness, is only possible in the name of Christ. To say that confession can have a

cathartic effect, providing relaxation, relief, and clarification, is not to imply that catharsis means only an abreaction of tensions, as many suppose. No, much more happens. Abreaction may enable the person to see his problems more objectively, get more self-knowledge, more self-acceptance. We speak of *confession* only when the confession of guilt occurs in the presence of God and his servant. It can be said that the relation between catharsis and confession may be compared with the relation between psychotherapy and pastoral care—not forgetting that, in spite of this differentiation, one may go over into the other.

2. The function of confession can be to transcend loneliness, especially that loneliness which is the consequence of sin. Sin makes lonely and, therefore, often goes together with anxiety. Confession may mean restoration of communion with God and the community. It could be said that psychotherapy means restoration in general and confession restoration with God and the brothers and sisters in Christ, the church. I have noticed that people do indeed experience differently the mentioning of exactly the same things in a therapeutic (possibly a cathartic) conversation and a confessional conversation.

3. Confessional conversation may be a help to overcome constraint and bondage. The person who struggles with serious sins in his life can have a very strong feeling of not being free. He feels that time and time again he does the same things in spite of himself. Regularly he is overcome by it. Sometimes he even experiences it as if he has the *will* to do differently but is *unable* to. In situations such as these the confessional conversation may help to overcome this constraint and bondage. Here we also find the transition from everyday problems to deep psychic conflicts, serious neurotic disturbances, and worse. As the personal lack of freedom in a neurotic form becomes more evident, as the neurosis colors the picture

198

more and more, confession alone, as a rule, will not be sufficient, but therapeutic help will also be necessary. It stands to reason that the pastor, in the first place, has to represent the love of God in all these situations, and should not start off with preaching the law of God; the person seeking help has probably already done this too much himself, and in the wrong manner! Two things should be avoided: a. excusing everything, by which no one is helped, b. the legalistic use of God's commandments. It is evident that only in a relationship where the person experiences the love of the pastor is there a possibility for further development in the pastoral conversation.

4. In confession it is the confessing of *guilt* that matters. With this we touch upon an important, but also an inexhaustable, psychological and theological problem. A few remarks, important within the framework of this chapter, will follow.

First of all, it is necessary to distinguish between a psychological and a theological approach to these questions. Psychologically, it is well to keep a number of differences in mind which can help us to approach the human reality with more awareness than is often the case. It is advisable to distinguish between a *consciousness* of guilt, that is, the *knowledge* of having done wrong, and a *feeling* of guilt, by which is meant the *suffering* of guilt feelings. These guilt feelings can be either more conscious or more unconscious; sometimes people smother in guilt feelings, even though they answer, when asked, that they don't have them.

We speak of genuine guilt feelings when those feelings are an adequate expression of the guilt which lies behind them. We speak of nongenuine guilt feelings, if a person indeed shows guilt feelings and possibly wants to have them but, in fact, is unable to experience his personal guilt adequately. Also the term *"infan-*

tile guilt feelings" is generally well-known, by which is meant a form of immature guilt feelings in which loss of love is predominantly feared. There is a feeling of inadequacy toward persons whose love is greatly valued and a fear that these persons will withdraw their love. It is not the real moral or religious value or act which matters, but the fear of being left alone, that the other person's love will no longer be received. Rümke stressed that, while infantile guilt feeling originates in a shortcoming of *received* love, mature guilt feeling (which he considers very difficult to define) is the consequence of a shortcoming in the *giving* of love. It is also remarkable that Rümke in this same connection says that mature guilt feeling seems to be very rare, even though it is quite possible, in his opinion, "that it occurs more often than we think, but that it is not as often mentioned to physicians and pastors as the infantile or pseudoguilt feeling." [4]

If we speak of guilt *theologically,* then we mean the failing of man toward God and his love. Guilt (German—Schuld) is etymologically related in German with "sollen" (morally obligated, must). It is something which can be demanded and in which a person falls short, for which he is punishable and may be held responsible. In this way *sin* (that is, not being able to stand before the Holy God, which is expressed in the condition of man—compare, for instance, Isa. 6—as well as in his actions) is imputed as guilt and demands reconciliation. This presumes a certain freedom and responsibility on the part of man. Furthermore, it would seem that the question of sin and guilt, in the theological sense, can properly be raised only when there is in one way or the other a

[4] "De verwerking van Schuldgevoel" (The Assimilation of Guilt Feeling), *Nieuwe Studies en Voordrachten over Psychiatrie (New Studies and Lectures on Psychiatry),* (Amsterdam, 1953), pp. 139 ff.

knowledge of God; only he can sin (and that is always sinning against God) who knows God.

It is important to be conscious of the guilt of man as a psychological problem, as a phenomenon in the eminent human sphere. For the Christian there is much more and something quite different. He knows he is standing *before God* with his guilt. He stands guilty before God's love, God's law, God's purpose with his life. Inasmuch as his guilt concerns things of the past, it cannot be changed or removed. No one can take back his thoughts, words, or deeds and undo them. Only God's forgiveness can restore and heal and make the impossible possible. It is God who justifies the ungodly, as it is formulated in the New Testament (Rom. 4:5). Here the words of absolution are heard: "Thy sins be forgiven."

Thus we can see that that which is important in confession and absolution is the knowledge of being completely accepted by God and our answer in faith, surrender, and love. The deepest human guilt is that we are unwilling to let God love us, and consequently we ourselves fall short in giving love toward our fellow man and, above all, toward God. Loving surrender to the fellow man and to God may lead to restoration of the communion with God.

Confronted with the guilt feelings which people frequently bring up in the confessional conversation, I should, in summary, like to stress the following viewpoints:

1. Regarding many guilt feelings about which people speak with the pastor, we have to be careful and should try to come to a carefully differentiated understanding.

2. The discussion of infantile and nongenuine guilt feelings as if they were mature and genuine guilt feelings may serve only to increase and intensify them.

3. Also, in pastoral practice it is important to reckon with the fact that, even after years, guilt feelings may break through.[5]

4. Where infantile guilt feelings are involved, they can block mature guilt feelings. Then it may happen that a person still feels very badly about masturbation as an unpardonable sin of youth but hardly experiences a horrible crime as guilt.

Now, can it be said that the fact that we psychologically account for the guilt of the person and the nature of his guilt feelings would discharge us from taking the theological appreciation seriously, from seeing these things in the light of faith? On the contrary! I would rather say that as we learn to think more clearly and with greater understanding, we will also come to greater clearness theologically. We can illustrate this by the following case.

A man tells the pastor his problem is that he continuously violates the fifth commandment and falls short in respect for his late father. This father, to whom he is neurotically attached, would never have approved that he purchased life insurance for his wife and children, had his children vaccinated, etc. His father had been fervently against such things as a sign of distrust in the providence of God, and always had urged him never to do them. Personally, the man has quite a different opinion, but on the other hand he experiences it as a heavy guilt against God and his father that he did not respect his father's will. The recognition of this psychological reality can keep the pastor from speaking of guilt theologically, at least in the way this man does. He who, without psychologically differentiating it, would immediately accept this confession at face value ("I continually sin against the fifth commandment and do not respect my deceased father") would say: "Yes, indeed, the person who does that stands guilty before God," but in

---

[5] Rümke, "Late werkingen van psychotraumata" (Late Effects of Psychotraumata), *Nieuwe Studies en Voordrachten*, p. 99.

this way the man would sink deeper and deeper in the morass of his infantile guilt feelings.

What is the relation between repentance and confession? In the first place, we should ask what is meant by repentance. The following elements should be considered as essential: a personal, free admission of certain acts as guilt and regretting them; the wish to return to the right way; the willingness to accept the consequences of what was done. But what about the relation between repentance and confession? An important question. Many pastors are of the opinion that one may confess only if he sincerely repents. And certainly during the confessional conversation repentance should be clearly evident.

Is this right? Is it not rather that repentance is something for which inner growth and maturing is necessary and that it only becomes possible in an atmosphere of love and acceptance? That is the reason why I should like to say that confessional conversation in many cases may not presuppose repentance, but rather has to lead to it. Therefore, the anxious watching of many pastors and other Christians to see whether somebody truly repents after a misstep, is to be rejected. Repentance needs as "soil" a communion of faith, hope, and love. It certainly should not be forced by letting the other person feel that it is resented if he does not repent enough.

It is in the confessional conversation, if anywhere, that it be discussed whether the pastor has something of the patient watchful love which Christ demands of us. In the confessional conversation a person may speak about the ugly, mean, sly things in his life about which perhaps nobody knows. Also about the things he does wrong time and time again. It is quite human that a pastor thinks: "This has to stop! If he takes his missteps seriously enough that he wishes to speak about them, then he should take the trouble to overcome them!" But let the pastor, when he feels this way, dive into

203

his own heart! It is necessary for the pastor to have a great deal of patience with the other person, just as much and as long as God has patience with us. By putting it this way, we immediately exclude that "weakness" is meant here. We shall have to reckon with the incapability of a person to behave immediately as he should, even though he has confessed. We shall also have to reckon with the fact that he is not as yet prepared to break with a certain sin. In one way it is a real problem for him, and he dislikes himself for it—for that reason he went to the pastor; but in another way this certain sinful situation has acquired such a power and significance that he cannot and will not as yet break with it—but how difficult it is to know to which extent he is "not willing" or "not able." Then the first confessional conversation will be followed by more, and in these conversations the free decisions of the other person have to be prepared, giving him time to grow toward it, and not forcing a decision.

It may be that the following consideration is of more importance for the Roman Catholic pastorate than for the Protestant. At any rate, I should like to point out that in the pastoral conversation the pastor must feel free in regard to the set, safe rules and regulations, inside of which Christians like to walk (or at any rate think the others should walk). The pastor should have the courage to enter into a really personal conversation, that is, to realize that this situation of this person is absolutely unique. It is, of course, impressive that so many Roman Catholic and Protestant theologians have given so much thought to what Christians have to do or do not have to do. And this gives many a feeling of safety and certainty— now we know what to do. But the real pastor will feel unhindered in regard to Christian regulations and opinions, and together with this person he will try to understand God's way in this situation. He ventures into this totally new, personal case.

During the past decades much has been said and published about confession. The Roman Catholic practice presents many theological and psychological problems today, as I see it. The uneasiness of many priests and laymen in regard to the present situation is considerable. I would not be surprised if during the next decades important changes would take place. The many articles in the Roman Catholic monthly *Dux,* an educational review, which more or less concern the problems discussed in this chapter, form one of the many symptoms of animated reflection. From the Protestant side there seems to be a growing call for the restoration of confession, partly due to a considerable amount of theological and psychological uncertainty.

In this situation, it seems important to ask whether we know what we really want. Do we want a regulated procedure of confession in which confession and absolution take place in an explicit liturgical form? Or do we want the confessional conversation, in which confession and absolution take place in the form of a pastoral conversation? Personally I prefer the latter, for two reasons in particular.

1. Our Protestant community lacks the conditions for a more regulated confessional practice (possibly also with a liturgical procedure). Proposals in this direction by a number of Protestants seem somewhat unreal and will probably not be realized anywhere.

2. This more regulated procedure of confessional practice is in danger of not doing justice to the person with his guilt in his particular situation. We know how necessary it is to discuss the problem of human guilt and all sorts of questions connected with it in a psychologically differentiated manner. This is only possible in the confessional *conversation* and often will require several conversations. When doing this, I think it is important that we practice the principles of conversation as extensively discussed in this

book. In other words, it is not a matter of the pastor making his diagnosis in a few moments and explaining to the other person to what extent he has infantile or mature guilt feelings, genuine or nongenuine feelings, etc. No, here again, we will help the other especially by means of a pastoral-therapeutic phase in which he comes to a clearer and a deeper insight into himself.

It is frequently asked whether a confessional conversation—by which we mean a conversation that a person seeks especially because of the distressing situation of his guilt—should not have a liturgical ending through prayer, the reading of the Bible, a word of absolution, or a blessing. Either all, or some of these, can be of great value, and the pastor should decide when and where they should be used. But it also presumes some understanding on the part of the other person! If we cannot expect this, it should be omitted. Otherwise, serious misunderstandings may arise, even after a good conversation. In practice this means that, at least in the present situation in the church, such a form often has to be omitted.

The Blessing

I have the impression that the blessing seldom has a place during the pastoral conversation, certainly in the Netherlands, even though there are pastors who are using it more or less in their pastoral work. I am inclined to say that we deprive people of that which most certainly can be of value to them. The blessing consists of spoken words (which can vary depending on the situation and which preferably are taken from the Bible and liturgical tradition) and an act (the hands are laid on the head). The latter is in the first place a symbolic expression of the communion of God with this person. It could be compared with the handshake between two people. Whereas the handshake expresses the communion between two equals, the laying on of hands expresses communion between someone who is superior—in this case, God—and the dependent person. The laying on of hands also symbolizes dedication to God, the person on whom the hands are laid is thereby dedicated to God. So the laying on of hands is a very meaningful symbolic act, which we know in the Protestant world on several occasions: with the blessing at the end of the service, at the wedding ceremony, with the confirmation of ministers, etc. Would it mean an enrichment also to give the blessing a place in the pastoral care to the individual? I believe that it would. Especially in the ministry of the ill and the dying or as the closing of a confessional conversation, it may have a meaningful place. It is an act derived from the Bible and the tradition of the church which also can be a blessing for modern man. But when the blessing is given, it should be done completely, by which I mean with physical contact. Therefore, please, no hands which float a few inches above the heads as it is sometimes seen at wedding ceremonies or at the ordination of elders. That is the same thing as shaking hands while leaving a couple of inches in between to avoid any physical contact. No, a handshake should be a physical act. In this way it creates a communion in a realistic manner. But the same is true for the laying on of hands in the blessing; the hands rest on the head while the mouth says the words. The two together form the act of healing, cleansing, forgiveness, encouragement, creating of communion, and, in all this, blessing.

Can and may we do this? In a way, no. "Only He can bless who has power. Only He can bless who can create. Only God can bless," as Romano Guardini says. But he continues by saying that "God authorized those who act in His place to give the blessing: the parents, the ministers of Christ's church, the believer.

207

To all those God gave the power to bless with His own life—to everybody in a different way according to their charge." [6]

It should be realized again here that the use of blessing in a pastoral relationship depends on whether the other person will have sufficient understanding for it. The religious climate of the other can be such that an act like this would absolutely not be understood.

For many people in the modern world, however, it is rare that a hand touches them lovingly and is laid in blessing on their heads. In our so keenly competitive world, in which we so often have to be hard-boiled in order to hold our own, and in which real attention and care for the other is often rare, hands frequently clench to fists, hands push away, hands often can disrespectfully and greedily grab and violate. For many there is seldom a hand that encouragingly, consolingly, lovingly is laid on the head. And how many men and women would not yearn for it? Some may regard this as a strange thought, but I am inclined to say: Would this not be a reason for the pastors to give more place to the laying on of hands?

The Bible and Other Literature

The reading of a part of the Bible can be a surprise in a pastoral conversation and bring in a totally new element. Many experience it as something quite unique, as something different from the word of the pastor.

We are thinking of the words of Jesus, "Where two or three have met together in my name, I am there among them." A pastoral conversation can offer such a situation in which two people, pastor and parishioner, meet with the Lord, and this may be expressed by reading or quoting the Bible. The other way around: The fact

[6] *Von heiligen Zeichen (On Holy Signs)*, (Mainz), pp. 47 ff.

that the Bible itself is introduced can clearly make the being together of two people into a communion in the name of the Lord. *How* the Bible is introduced is another question. In many cases it will be best to read the Bible. It is well to take the spiritual background of the person in question into account when choosing a translation. It may be well to use an old Bible translation in the contact with a very traditional church member. In other cases it may be more appropriate to use a newer translation. Generally speaking, the reading should be kept short. Of course, it is necessary that the pastor shall have such knowledge of the Bible that he have those parts at his disposal which are applicable in different situations.

Apart from the actual reading of the Bible, quoting a few words of the Scriptures can also be of significance, as can reference to a certain story or parable. A good example of quoting the Bible is the following:

A pastor is visiting a very ill man, about forty years of age, who is dying. During the last visit that he makes, he enters the sickroom, finds the patient very exhausted, and says, "Mr. Johnson, is there anything that I can do for you, or would you like to say something?"

Patient: "Thank you, Reverend. . . . Not now. . . . I am so tired."
Pastor: (standing near the patient and looking quietly at him) "Jesus Christ said: Come to me all whose work is hard, whose load is heavy, and I will give you relief."
Patient: (with a radiant, peaceful expression on his face) "Thank you, Reverend." [Pastor leaves.]

When the next-of-kin visited him that evening, the patient told them how thankful he was for the word of the Bible that the pastor had given him. He passed away that same night.

The reading of the Bible in the pastoral contact also evokes something of a shift in the relationship. During the conversation there was a certain asymmetry between the partners: on the one hand there was the parishioner who came to the pastor; on the other hand there was the pastor who gave the parishioner his time. The moment the Bible is read a certain change will take place. Even though the pastor reads, he and the parishioner are in a very similar position, because both of them are addressed by the same word of the Lord. Both participate in the same listening attitude to what God has to say. Both are drawn into the dialogue between God and his children. As a consequence the pastor who has explicitly given a place to the word of the Bible does something which will distract attention away from his own person, will prevent too strong a dependency upon him, and will explicitly refer to God. The pastor who does not only speak about God in his own words, but who also uses the words of the Bible itself, may be experienced to a greater extent as the servant of God, whose word he may proclaim, to whom he may refer.

It hardly needs to be said that the pastor who directly introduces the words of the Bible into a pastoral conversation should do this only after he has listened very closely to his partner, so that he will choose those words which will be understood by the other in his situation. For the risk of misuse of the Bible in the pastoral conversation is not a trifling matter. Indeed, the use of the Bible has to be justified; that is to say, the part of the Bible that is read must do justice to this conversational situation. It should be remembered that the appeal to the formal authority of the Bible loses more and more of its value for people of today. It has estranged many from the pastorate of the Christian church. For this reason the Bible should never be read in the pastoral conversation in such a way as to imply that it is the word of God to which man has to submit himself. Simply reading the Bible is the most advisable way, without explicit claims to authority. Then the other person will *discover* what power these words have for him.

As to the advice to personally read the Bible, that also is a matter of great importance. But in many cases the other person will need much help and instruction to *learn* to read the Bible. Much depends on the place the reading of the Bible has had so far in a person's life. Let us have no illusions about it—the individual reading of the Bible occurs much less (even among parishioners) than the large number of Bibles which are in circulation would suggest. The reading of the Bible has become a problem for many people in and outside of the church. Therefore, to bridge the gap between pastoral conversation and personal Bible reading demands the attention of the pastor to determine in what way he can be of service to this certain person in this matter.

Besides the Bible, something different may well be read in a given situation during the pastoral conversation: A certain piece of meditative literature, a poem, etc. This not only depends on the conversational situation but also what the pastor has at his immediate disposal. Another more modern instrument which I myself sometimes use is the record player or the tape recorder, if something suitable is on it. Sometimes during a pastoral conversation the pastor may feel: Better than I myself could say it, it may become more clear to the other by playing a certain song. Again, the pastor has to understand the person's feelings and should not play his own favorites which the other person perhaps does not appreciate at all. But, if it is the right choice, God's word may come through to a person in the pastoral conversation by means of a song or something else.

211

Form and Freedom in the Use of Religious Resources

Throughout this chapter we have again and again touched upon an important aspect of the pastoral conversation. The pastor should feel *free* to say and do what is most effective in a given situation. For certain stages and situations in the pastoral contact, the nondirective method is an excellent expedient; perhaps we may say: *the* method marked out for it. Then the method has to be used in the right way. But for the rest, the pastoral conversation should be characterized by a great measure of freedom, the freedom to do everything by which the other will be helped—to pray with him but also to listen to a record or a tape recording, to refer to the church service or the Bible group but also to the film or the theater where something is presented that probably will mean something to him in his situation. This stressing of freedom in the pastoral conversation does not mean taking a stab at it, neither is it a justification for arbitrariness. On the contrary, it is the very idea that even our improvisation is the result of patient listening and a corresponding creative response.

The freedom of pastoral conversation may also be observed in the time and place in which it occurs. As a rule, the pastoral conversation will take place by appointment in the office of the pastor or at the home of the parishioner. But a pastoral conversation may also start in a sidewalk cafe, drinking a cup of coffee, or while the minister chats with one of the young people at a party. Experience has taught us that many—especially young people—find it difficult to make a special appointment, but actually they do want to have a talk with their pastor. All at once, in an informal situation they will start speaking about their problems.

There is a question which regularly comes up and about which I should like to make a few special remarks: Should Bible reading and prayer have a place in home calls (often as its closing), especially in those parishes or with those parishioners where it is *expected*? It is well known that for many a pastor this is a problem. It is often felt that it has no meaning in the conversational context. The conversation, which centered on everyday trifles and had no depth, did not lead up to it. But in spite of this, it is expected that at the closing of the home call, the pastor will read from the Bible and a prayer will be said. If it is not done, it may be very much resented. Indeed, the key here is to be found in the expectations of the home. Where Bible reading is not expected as a matter of course, it should not be done unless it is clearly evident from the conversational situation that it is desirable. Through the course of years I have heard many parishioners report that the experience of Bible reading and prayer can be a most disturbing—if not immodest—element of a home call, with which they felt ill at ease. So it should be said: Don't do it, if there is no clear motive for it.

Apart from this, I am of the opinion that where parishioners *expect* it (quite often this is easy to tell because this is a regular use in a certain community), the pastor as a rule may fulfill this expectation. Considerations such as—It is only "tradition," the conversation had so little content—are in my opinion insufficient counterarguments. In the form of this "tradition" a truly pastoral conversation may be had, in spite of the lack of personal openness at the home call. This all depends on the manner in which the pastor switches from the possibly trivial conversation to "the liturgy of the home community" (this should be done in a clear and simple fashion) and the way in which he then proceeds. Certainly the pastor should make no effort to try to say in prayer what he could not say in the conversation. It is advisable that he have a set of prayers at his disposal which he can say in such a case. Otherwise, it is extremely easy, especially if the conversation offers no background, to fall back on the saying of "religious" commonplaces.

Generally, I have the impression that pastors often underestimate the religious importance of Bible reading and prayer in situations as discussed above. Probably the "tradition" which we look down upon may have a truly religious meaning for the person involved.

The Call for Pastoral Conversation

The gradually increasing number of publications in this field and the interest of more and more pastors and their coworkers show that more and more people realize the great importance of the matters which have been discussed and advocated in this book. It is of the greatest importance that university and church shall give ample room to this development in the future. Reflection upon, and education for, the pastoral conversation must have a central place in the life and work of the church, because in the pastoral conversation it is God himself who continues his dialogue with men throughout the ages. The Scriptures tell us that Jesus Christ was moved with compassion over the multitude which he saw as sheep without a shepherd (Matt. 9:36). He keenly and fully saw the need and loneliness in which so many are lost without being in any way aware of shelter, of guidance, of an aim in their life. And just as in those days, so now he also asks us whether we are willing to go out to our fellow man to serve him, not only with our hands but also with our hearts, in our communication with him, our dialogue in and through which this fellow human may be helped to see his life, his joys and sorrows in God's light.

It is evident that many people are in desperate need. Man today —in his work, in his marriage and family, in his single state, in the many forms of social life in which he moves, in his scientific work, in his leisure hours—often feels himself at the mercy of forces from within and without himself which he can barely cope with, if indeed he is not completely overwhelmed.

In this situation it is of immense importance that the irreplaceable significance of the pastoral conversation shall again be recognized as a commandment of the Lord and a blessing for innumerable people.

index

217